TURNING BACK THE PAGES OF TIME

Volume II

Ellen (Thompson) Graves

Copyright © 2011 by Ellen Graves

All rights reserved. No part of this publication may be reproduced, stored in a retrieval system or transmitted in any form or by any means, electronic, mechanical, photocopying, recording or otherwise, without the prior written permission of the publisher.

Published by Sedona Heritage Publishing

Layout and Cover design by William and Francine Levengood

Printed in the United States of America

Front Cover: *Red Rock. Fred Schuerman, Ellen and Paul Thompson in wagon Fred built and the playhouse Fred and friend built.*

Turning Back the Pages of Time II

TABLE OF CONTENTS

GREAT 1938 FLOOD PLUS THREE OTHER FLOODS	4
HISTORY OF FRANK JACKSON AND FAMILY AND OTHERS.	12
MOSTLY ABOUT PARTNERSHIP OF ED BLACK AND FRANK JACKSON TOLD BY FRANK	23
RED ROCK SCHOOL	29
THIS IS A SHORT CHAPTER MADE UP OF RED ROCK SCHOOL NEWS 1942-43	42
MORE RED ROCK SCHOOL AND AREA SCHOOLS	45
EXCERPTS FROM LETTERS	52
EARLY YEARS OF ALBERT AND MABEL AND FAMILY AT RED ROCK	63
WORLD WAR II AT RED ROCK	73
EVENTS AT RED ROCK AND SAMUEL ALBERT ARRIVES	78
INTERESTING WEATHER AND A FOREST FIRE	84
FAMILY FUN AND ENJOYMENT	89
MORE RED ROCK MEMORIES	99
R.E.A. POWER COMPANY RACE	108
OUR NEW TRACTOR AND PESKY CALF	117
RED ROCK AND OUR NEIGHBORS	120
THE AREA AROUND RED ROCK	128
PEOPLE WE VISITED AT RED ROCK	137
OUR LAST YEARS AT RED ROCK	141
YEARLY CHORES	143
FARM PROJECTS	149
OTHER RED ROCK ACTIVITIES	150
MOVING DAY DRAWS NEAR	155

CHAPTER 1

GREAT 1938 FLOOD PLUS THREE OTHER FLOODS

All the old timers referred to the 1938 flood as the big flood of 38. Information came from several sources which I give as I go along. Twin brother Paul and I weren't a year old in March 38, so we don't remember it. Mom and Dad told stories about it, as did other people. A family friend, Mr. Bouton, helped half-brother, Fred Schuerman, build a playhouse from lumber washed down from the Purtymun chicken house above Indian Gardens.

In March of 38, both Oak Creek and Munds Creek, which runs into Oak Creek above Indian Gardens, were very high. The flood was caused by wet snow three to five feet deep in the rim country. Early in March it began to rain and lasted three days.

Dick Russell gave some information. He was present when Ed and Maggie Van Deren's tent house, below Jesse and Lizzie Purtymun's house washed away. They had a little warning and were able to get out with a few belongings and daughter, Margaret and baby Don. Ed took his old hat because it was raining, so his new hat floated away. The tent house washed into the deep hole below what it now called the Point. Vera Purtymun Hedges, half-sister of Maggie, told me she and Maggie went down creek looking for belongings but found nothing of value. The big kitchen range in the tent was never

Turning Back the Pages of Time II

found. When Ed built his house, it was on a hill across the highway. It was above Elmer and Iva Purtymun's house. Maggie and Iva were sisters. The whole area is now the Red Rock Motel.

Rest of Great Flood of 1938 taken from Bud James Purtymun's "Arches of Time".

Not only Edwin and Maggie Van Deren's tent house washed away according to Bud. His brother Elmer and Iva Purtymun weren't on high ground either. They built a small cabin close to the creek on Jesse's land. Jesse had cleared land and planted trees near there. The creek was high so everyone was up during the night checking on Elmer's house and the tent house. At day light, the Van Deren's tent house floated through Jesse's new berry and fruit orchard. It came apart in the main current after getting out of creek bottom trees.

Elmer's house was on stilts near a bank. The water cut away the bank and the house fell. No wonder both families rebuilt on much higher ground.

A family that lived across from Midgley Bridge was water bound by Oak Creek and Bear Wallow. Ira Smith and another man took groceries by horse back when it was safe to cross. They found the family all right.

Both Indian Garden Bridge and the bridge at the John Loy home in Munds Park on Schnebley Hill Road went out. Jess Purtymun rebuilt both.

The course of the creek was changed and ditches had to be mostly rebuilt. Deep holes were gone and some shallow ones became deep. The Sedona School closed for several days. Teachers and some students lived on the east side of the creek. Teachers lived at Bill Steele's ranch. Some water bound students were Charley Thompson's girls, the Fred Hart family and the Lee Piper family.

Sedona had a black iron bridge and water slopped over it. A lot of the road to the west washed away leaving only big river boulders. Six or seven feet of water had flooded the area where Tlaquepaque and other buildings are now.

I remember the iron bridge with creek bottom trees around it.

Laura McBride gave me the next information.

Where Munds Creek enters Oak Creek above Indian Gardens, Munds Creek over ran its banks and down over Greene and Gertrude Thompson's land. Their house was in the Bacon Rind Park area. They awoke to water pouring through their house and big logs hitting the sides of it. They were able to grab baby Gloria and get to dry land, but lost all they owned. Brother Albert loaned them items to set up housekeeping from his cabin. He was just glad they were safe. Greene rebuilt several feet higher and nearer the highway and was safe. A two-story log cabin is on the site now. Big trees kept the Thompson house from going down creek, so he used the lumber to rebuild.

Turning Back the Pages of Time II

The flood had closed Highway 89A, so Uncle Greene parked his car crossways in the highway, not knowing a slide would come down and bury part of it. The rain and snow caused mud and rock slides throughout areas of the canyon. A big slide came off Wilson Mountain at Indian Gardens and caved in part of the dance hall and then crossed the highway. The water also crossed the road and the bridge went out. Before it went out, the county had dedicated the road so Jesse Purtymun got paid to rebuild the bridge. There are still remains of the old concrete abutments on the east side above present ones. Jesse added a concrete pier in the middle as well as on each side. The above information came from Bud Purtymun's book, "Arches of Time".

There were parts of the highway that were washed away. It was washed out south of Mission Rancho and above Junipine. One year I went to high school, and half the road above Junipine washed away. At the October 5, 2008 picnic, Mary Wyatt told me the following: Her family, Ira, Elsie and Mary Smith were living in the canyon at the present Mission Rancho. Her Mother said she did not want to be there in another flood. Part of the highway crew came along, Ira could see the road better than the crew, so he was able to warn them the road was washed out.

Laura McBride's parents, Albert and Clara Purtymun and younger children, Bud, Charley and Zola had a small place with a cabin where the Manzanita campground is. In the flood the chicken houses and barn and most of the orchard went down creek.

There had been a steady rain and the creek was already high. It poured all night and about 10 a.m., it really poured. All the family had gone to see the big falls down creek. It was likely that 2 1/2 year old Gwendolyn stayed with Laura and Grandma Purtymun. Laura was very pregnant with expected Ted Ray in April. The banks started to cave in and Papa and the others showed up to help save animals and belongings. A neighbor, Tom Quick, who lived above them, lost half the flat he was living on.

Ray McBride's Dad, Dave McBride, and an old friend were living below Uncle Charley Thompson on the west side of the creek near Bedside Manor. Ray waded to rescue the men and by the time all got to land, the water was only about 15 feet from his cabin to the creek.

After the flood, a neighbor Mr. and Mrs. McDowell, who lived south of Pendley's, said he saw trout tossed up to 20 feet in alder trees by their home. Laura said Mrs. McDowell was a kind sweet old lady with snow-white hair. She would ring a bell, and they would take care of her.

Uncle Frank Thompson and Aunt Hilda lived across from where McBride's built their house. Being water bound, he climbed the Thompson Ladder trail and crossed Bee and other canyons until he got to the trail that went down by Pendley Bridge. Meeting the highway crew, he got a job. He walked down the road until he was across from his

Turning Back the Pages of Time II

house and went to the creek. There, he tossed notes around rocks to Aunt Hilda until she got one telling her of his job. Hilda was afraid of the swinging bridge, later built, and never used it.

Mary Wyatt also told me that the forest lease below Uncle Charlie's, before you get to Grasshopper Point, had a lot of damage. Avis Thompson's parents Ruben and Vera Hedges and some of the family, lived there.

Mary's Uncle Fred and Nellie Hart's place below Sedona Bridge wasn't washed away. However, when he showed a man driftwood in the creek bottom 20 feet in the trees, the man would not believe water got that high.

I talked to half-brother Fred Schuerman, and Sherman Loy when I talked to Mary. They said nobody lost home or property in Red Rock. It is possible that because in an earlier flood in February 1920, their Grandparent's, Henry Sr. and Doretta Schuerman lost all land away from well built rock house, a quarter of a mile from the creek. They rebuilt near Red Rock Road. Both Fred and Sherman said an old place below Red Rock suffered damage.

Charley Thompson had his post office across the creek from his ranch so the mail carrier would not have to cross a flooded creek. In the big flood of 38, the basement flooded, so Charley moved the post office to up town Sedona.

Ellen Graves

After Laura and Ray McBride bought their property from Greene and Gertrude Thompson and built their house, they found a big drift above their house with lots of rattlesnakes in it. A big pine that came down in the flood caused the drift. They built their cabin and later added on. They moved lumber from her parent's house up the creek. Laura enjoyed bringing creek bottom rocks up so Ray suggested she put them on the house and she added pretty rocks, glass and relics. She put rocks for a wall by the creek side and wall behind the house, and put in grass and flowers.

Now I will tell of an earlier and later flood. My cousin Verna's husband, Dick Russell, told that in 1921 the dam broke at the head of Munds Creek in Munds Park and a terrible flood came down the canyon into Oak Creek. Both he and my Dad, Albert Thompson, said it was the highest they ever saw Munds Creek. Dick told a tale on brothers Earl and Burrell. The Russell family, Oscar and Nell and boys, lived in Sedona The boys thought it would be fun to see if horses could swim in the flood, so they pushed some in. It was likely the boys were frightened when the horses were bowled over by the flood waters and went rolling down the creek for some distance until they got ashore. If the creek had not been so high they could have swam out with little trouble. At least once Ray and Laura McBride's milk cow Beu, short for Beauty, swam Oak Creek in the flood.

In 1966, once again there was fear the Munds Creek dam would break and take out Freeway 17.

Turning Back the Pages of Time II

There was talk of using dynamite to prevent the road from going out. There was water backed onto the golf course, and a backhoe was mostly under water. My husband, Nelson Graves, was working for the Arizona Highway Department building the freeway through the Arizona Strip that goes from California through Nevada, Utah and into Canada. We and children, Jack and June, lived at St. George, Utah. Twin brother Paul and Cora Mae and Joe, Paula and Ann moved into our house overnight because it was on much higher ground than their house. Luckily the people in charge got it under control or a lot of homes would have been washed away in the canyon and Sedona.

When we returned to the canyon sometime in the 70's, another big flood came. People were warned but a woman died when she drove her car into the creek at the Trout Farm dip, below Indian Gardens. In Sedona several trailers washed away in the area above the Chavez crossing dip. Brother Fred Schuerman, Paul and Nelson looked for salvage. Paul did ok with a bathtub boat, but it sank with Nelson.

Another time when the creek wasn't so high, Bill and Gwen Towne and Nelson rafted from Steele's trailer Park in Sedona and went below the bridge.

Ellen Graves

CHAPTER 2

HISTORY OF FRANK JACKSON AND FAMILY AND OTHERS.

FRANK JACKSON WITH SONS, WESLEY AND SKIKEE (FRANK, JR.)

Turning Back the Pages of Time II

I interviewed Frank Jackson at his Indian Gardens store before he and Wesley sold to Bill Garland. Wesley gave some information.

Benjamin Franklin (Frank) Jackson's father's name was James A. Jackson. The family moved from Texas to Phoenix when Frank was eight in 1918 at almost the end of the year.

Frank went to Alhambra Phoenix School his first year of school. In 1920 he went to Wickenburg School. In 1922, he went to the old Willard school in Bridgeport, a section of Cottonwood. In 1923, he attended the Sedona School. Frank's Dad was a carpenter and he helped build the first bridge over the Verde River at Bridgeport in 1919. Sedona had a bridge over Oak Creek before the Verde Bridge was built.

The Jackson's had a homestead in Grasshopper Flats, West Sedona. Frank attended the Sedona School in 1923 and went through 1925. The last day of school was May, 1925. His teacher was Miss Sally Hudspeth who was Mrs. George Black later. All three school trustees were from Sedona. Having no trustee they had no "say so" about school affairs. Frank's Dad did not like that, so Mr. Jackson started working to get a school in Grasshopper Flats. He contacted Mrs. Archebeau, the Yavapai School Superintendent, and they got together. She said there was no money for a school, but if he would build one furnishing the labor, he might get paid later. James Jackson donated two acres of his homestead for the school. Being a carpenter by trade, he built the school, and it was ready on September 26, 1926. Georgia Hudspeth, sister of Sedona's teacher Sally Black, was teacher. The community called the women Miss Sally and Miss Georgia because they were from Baton Rouge, La.

My folks told me an interesting story about Miss Georgia. It seemed that in sewing some item of clothing, she stuck a needle in her foot and couldn't get it out. Supposedly, several years later, it came out her knee.

Frank said there were 16 children that first year. The Coleman's lived at Soldiers' Basin on Soldiers' Pass Road. The Jackson children were Louise, Katherine, Ed and Frank. Malcolm Nickelson was another child Frank remembered the name of. There were more kids from the Flats in 1927 than 1926. The school became known as the Jackson School and was District 26. The school at Red Rock was District 27. When Jackson deeded the school to the county, he stipulated that if the schoolhouse was moved from the land, the land returned to him or his heirs. When they did move the school in the 1940,s Mrs. Jackson got the property. As a child, I remember seeing the school when it no longer was used. Mr. Jackson was a religious man, so he also stipulated the school could only be used for school or church activities. He relented and two dances were held there. At one dance, a lot of people came. Another time Guy and Greene Thompson came and asked to have a dance, as there had been a disagreement at the Sedona School. The Jackson's were Baptists and wanted no dances or card playing.

Turning Back the Pages of Time II

In 1929 or 1930, Miss Greene was teacher and in the early 30's, Mrs. Bunger taught. Ellen Grant also taught and there were two or three more.

Frank's son, Wesley, said he had Miss Freestone and Matty Evans, possibly others, Mrs. Riordan and Alfred Wohslegel. Until the Sedona School burned down from lightening caused fire in summer of 48, Mrs. Lydia Brewer, known affectionately as Ma Brewer, was cook and nurse at the school. Mrs. Brewer and her husband, Charley, lived in a house with land at the end of Brewer Road. They had sons, Laurel, Furn, Sox, Buzz, and Arley Jack, and two daughters, Sylvia and Tootie. My Dad knew the family when all were home and sometimes ate with them. Lots of beans, potatoes and biscuits were served to fill those hungry boys. The wooden building where Mrs. Brewer cooked was called the cook shack.

When the Indian Gardens Restaurant opened in Jackson's store, Mrs. Brewer cooked delicious meals there for a time.

The summer after the fire at the school, they were able to build enough rooms for the younger grades. Until just before Christmas, the 5th and 6th grades taught by Mrs. Riordan, and the 7th and 8th grades taught by Principal Alfred Wohslegel were in two rooms at the Ranger Station garage. Mr. Wohslegel was Mrs. Carl Mayhew's son-in-law, and sometimes helped at the lodge. Wesley told me that the in fall of 49, the 8th grade was moved to Flagstaff and he, Minnie Steele, possibly Wesley's friend, Bud Mosley, went to Flagstaff. Paul and I went to Sedona from 5th grade to 8th grade May 1951.

A picture was taken of Mrs. Riordan's 5th and 6th grade in the 1947-48 school years. It had Paul, Ellen, and Cousins Carol, Charlotte Ruth, Charles Ruben Thompson, also cousins Ted McBride, Fred Fuentes, and Don Van Deren in the 5th grade. Others were Wayne Fuqua, Orville Wester, Vernon and Fred Coleman and sister, Emma Jean and Don Newton, all in the 5th grade. 6th grade Ted Blem, Minnie Steele, Bud Mosley, Walter Jordan, Jr. and Wesley Jackson. Mrs. Elsie Riordan looked very pretty.

Frank Jackson got part of his information from the Phoenix, Arizona School archives and he said it is a good place to get school information.

School history mainly by Ruth Jordan:

Mrs. Ruth Jordan, my beloved Red Rock teacher of 1946-1947, the last school year held there, gave me this following Sedona School information. (The Red Rock School started fall of 1891 and ended spring of 1946.)

A Mrs. Venda Sides was a teacher in Sedona in 1930 or 31. She was very popular among the young people and parents. She attended a literary society that Ruth and Helen Jordan started that met once a month at the school. There was another teacher from Flagstaff named Charlotte from a well-known family she did not remember. One year, there were three teachers and one was a young man. All the teachers visited her in her Sedona cabin about 1934. Later, the young man almost died of appendicitis. He drove himself either to the Jerome or Flagstaff hospital and was never well again. His sister sent doll furniture to Ruth's girls, Ann and Ruthie. Stanton Wallace was another teacher. His family and the Schnebly's were old friends and he married the youngest Schnebly girl. She was in about the 9th grade when he taught. Mr. and Mrs. Freestone had two children. They probably started 9th grade in the 1930,s. The family was very community minded.

Matty Evans taught in the 30,s or early 40,s and came back and taught a year or two before Mrs. Jordan, probably in the late 30's. Mrs. Brewer was cook and custodian. There were two teachers. Lois Price had upper grades, Mrs. Jordan 4th and 5th, and probably Mrs. Johnson primary.

I believe Dolly Schuerman taught and after 1945 another fine teacher was Mrs. Oma Bird. In 1947-48, the first year Paul and I attended the Sedona School, Mrs. Olsen, Ranger Merle Olsen's wife, had the youngest grades and Mrs. Bird taught 3rd and 4th grades. Mrs. Elsie Riordan had 5th and 6th and likely Mr. Wohslegel taught 7th and 8th. Some of the graduates from the 8th grade were Jean Olsen, Gene Bird, and Charlene Thompson.

Mrs. Jordan said it was a joy to teach the children because they were the best that ever were. In later years, she taught because teachers were scarce even though she had not renewed her certificate.

Ellen Graves

Big accomplishments at Sedona School follow: The school was the center of activities so the men of the community built the gymnasium where basketball games were played and games and plays sometimes dances. Mrs. Jordan told of a community event she remembered early in 1933. The people who took part were Mrs. Sedona Schnebly, Mrs. Van Deren, Mrs. Lydia Brewer, and Helen and Ruth Jordan. The name of the play was "Old Maids' Convention". In the play, the people went through a time machine and were rejuvenated.

At the Literary Society meetings, most of the women in the community and the teachers from Sedona and West Sedona went to monthly meetings at the school. Each month, there was a program - plays poems, and singing.

Ann and Ruthie weren't in school yet when the Freestone's were there, but they said nursery rhymes and acted them out. There would be from three to six people taking part. All the family from tots to Grandparents took part. They played baseball at school and the 9th graders and others, including Mary Ball and Bill Greene, played.

One Halloween, they had a spook house at school. Mrs. Jordan took part during recess and during school and had games for all the community. She was in charge of games, and one time 118 people were playing all together. Other than the Assembly of God, there were no churches in Sedona, so at the school or someone's house was where people met for Sunday school and Church. One of our early-day Red Rock teachers took us to

Turning Back the Pages of Time II

the Sedona School to Sunday school. Mrs. Jordan was our teacher. We studied about Moses and colored a fiery cloud and Moses and the people.

While at Red Rock, we went to a Halloween Party at the Sedona School and Ted McBride was dressed as a monkey. Another time, we attended a play at Sedona and cousins Stella Mae and Josephine were in it.

Before the school and gym burned, the Cottonwood Theatre showed movies on weekends at the school. Paul and I sometimes could get Brother Fred to bring us from Red Rock to a show. After we moved to the canyon, Cousin Laura sometimes took Paul &Ted, and sometimes Gwen down. We had cartoons and continued shows. One was a pretty jungle girl, ads and main attraction. Some shows I remember were "Peg of my Heart", "Mother Goes to College", and "Family Honeymoon" with Fred McMurry and I think Claudette Colbert.

Three of Miss Woolf's first pupils on Beaver Creek were little Sue Mercer, Emmett McMinamon and Zeke Taylor

When Paul and I went to school in Sedona, the school had a ball team that played other schools. Some of the boys on the team were Gene Bird and Walter Van Deren. The girls were Beverly Van Deren and Betty Passmore, and they were very good. Lovella Brewer played also.

Ellen Graves

The school took part in a track meet in the years of 1947-48 that was held at Flagstaff High School in the spring. Some of our kids did very well, like Fred and Vernon Coleman, Walter Van Deren, Gene Bird and Gloria Thompson. I did not do well in either jumping or the relay race. It was fun to take part. Aunt Gertrude took Gloria and me to Flagstaff.

Mrs. Riordan, our teacher, also taught music. She played piano and taught us cowboy and popular music, the Arizona state song and songs from our songbook. She was in charge of school programs for the whole school. On Christmas, 1947, there was a play and I was Mrs. Santa Claus. Gene Pirtle was Santa. A lot of kids were dressed as toys. Emma Jean Coleman was Raggedy Ann and danced with Raggedy Andy, redheaded Orville Wester. Younger children had a program. We all sang carols and ended with everybody singing cowboy songs, dressed in jeans and hats.

All the teachers in the early grades read books to us after recess, a chapter a day, usually for one half-hour. I enjoyed most stories Mrs. Riordan let us bring books and we read Zane Grey, Nancy Drew and the Hardy Boys among others.

Mrs. Claude Thompson was the first Sedona School teacher in 1910. Some later teachers were Ellen Clark, Dotty Hotchkiss, Charley Stemmer, Edith Lamport and Gladys Mumford. The first school in 1910 was one room about 14'x 15'. The outside of the building was so covered with brush, you couldn't see it.

Albert Thompson gave that information.

Turning Back the Pages of Time II

Dad, uncles, several cousins, Paul and I and Sam got to graduate from the Brewer Road School. All my seven children, Samantha & Aaron Thompson and some of Fred's children, and Joe and Paula Thompson got to attend the Sedona School. Five of my children, June, Ben, Matt, Ruth and Judy graduated. Jack, my oldest graduated from church school and Laurel, my youngest, had to go to West Sedona as did Samantha and Aaron. That was because in about 1994-95, the school district made the Brewer School into administrative offices and all children went to V.O.C. or West Sedona. At her graduation, all Laurel's brothers and sisters were there to cheer her on.

At Red Rock and Sedona, we had a lending library and books were brought from the county library to check out. Also at Red Rock and Sedona, the county nurse weighed and measured us, gave us shots and checked vision and hearing. At Sedona, once a week, two teachers that taught art and music came down from Flagstaff. Bessie Kidd Best, Flagstaff County School Superintendent, came once or twice a year and told us about children at Grand Canyon and little Indian children at Leupp.

Some of the teachers my children had at Sedona were Miss Baker, Mrs. Riordan, Mr. Taylor and Don Kelsey, Mrs. Thelma Fisher, Mrs. Peggy Mason, Sylvia Daily, John Kline, Kriss Nefstead, Mr. West, Vance Carter. The last principal and teacher, were Wanda James and Susan Myers, her secretary. Sue Pelekeske was bus driver.

Ellen Graves

Sedona School went from 1910 until 1992-93. The graduating class of the last year were, Becky Ellis, Kelly Roberts, Bill Robinson, Denise Waltz, Mike Cook, Natala Tingle, Judy Graves, Shay Sletman, Sarah Minnick, Sarah Thompson, Jonathan Borsee, James Sallee, Clint Stephens, Joah Thide, Sarah Curtis, Zack Allen, Clint Jackson, Matt Biddle, Sean Murry, and Dain Santee.

In 1991, my daughter, Ruth Graves, was valedictorian of her Sedona 8t grade class. A few of her classmates were Kenneth Lamb, Amy Householder, Wolfie Sukut, Katrina Wallace, Stephanie Brueland and Willie Garland.

Lydia Brewer cooked at Sedona School until the school burned. I went to school there after the school burned. The first year, my Aunt, Avis Thompson, had as assistant, Lydia Brewer's daughter-in-law, Ollie Brewer, son Laurel's wife. Avis let me work helping clean up the kitchen, and I earned lunch for Paul and me. Avis and Ollie were a lot of fun. Ollie showed the big girls how to dance the 20,s dance, the Charleston.

The next cook was Mrs. Hazel Miller and her husband Ralph, related to the Schnebly's, was custodian. Both were fine people. Mrs. Garbarino, whose husband had the garage in town, was assistant cook. I earned meals for me that year. The Millers had three sons, Gene, Darrell and Jack, and one daughter, Linda, who married my cousin, Don Van Deren, and is still a fine friend to Paul, Cora Mae and me.

CHAPTER 3

MOSTLY ABOUT PARTNERSHIP OF ED BLACK AND FRANK JACKSON TOLD BY FRANK

Frank Jackson went to work for George Black on May 11, 1925 the year he turned 15 in the fall. He and Ed Black, George's son, did farm work at what is now Poco Diablo Resort in Sedona. Ed was 19. The young men soon became close friends. Both lads began work for "Dad", L.E. Hart and Aunt Delia. They were friends all their lives and partners much of that time.

Frank thought the Hart's bought the store in 1926 from Lee Van Deren. Before that, Morgan Thompson, no kin of J.J. Thompson, ran the store. Dad Hart came from Kansas, and Mrs. Hart from Wisconsin. When the Hart's came to Arizona, he was in the cow business around Flagstaff. He ran and was superintendent of the Poor Farm, now a historical museum in Flagstaff.

At this time, Hart's Store was under the hill on Soldier's Wash near the bridge to Brewer School. At that time, the road through Sedona was a dirt road going from Grasshopper Flats, taking off by the airport hill and coming down behind the Sedona School. It connected with the Big Park road and on to upper Sedona and Flagstaff. I remember when you could drive between the school and Cook Hill.

Ellen Graves

T.C. Schnebly was the caretakers at the CCC camp in Sedona after it closed down. While the camp was going, during the Depression years, there were 200 men and they changed every so often. The men traded at Hart's Store, and it kept the store going. The payroll was $6000 and each man got $30 a month. Most of it was sent home to the families. There were Forest Service men, Federal Government bosses and overseers also. CCC men mostly worked on erosion control and roads and trails.

Frank first worked for Hart's under the hill. It was February 8, 1930 when he was 20. Ed Black had worked there since 1929. The boys worked for Hart's for seven years until the store was moved after Highway 89A came through Sedona, and the old store was no longer on the road.

While working for Hart's, Frank and Ed cleared the land where the new store was built. There were only a couple of shacks there when they cleared out the rocks and trees. They used a team of horses and a rock boat. Hart's store opened in 1938 and Ed and Frank leased it from them. A basement was built under the store at the time it was built. In 1940, the men added a rock addition on the east side of the store for an eating place and liquor store. Katharine Smith was a waitress there. Dad Hart saw it was a good business, so he paid them for it and charged them rent. The cold box was built with the original store. An add on for a feed store was built later.

Once in a while when we lived at Red Rock, Dad got ice and the folks made ice cream for a summer

Turning Back the Pages of Time II

treat. There was a gas station outside. The Trailways bus stopped there.

Black and Jackson decided it would be a good idea to have a business at Indian Gardens. At the first of the year in 1942, they leased the dance hall at Indian Gardens from Jim and Guy Thompson. They also leased the cabins and turned the dance hall into a skating rink. The partners dissolved their partnership. Frank sold his part of the Sedona business to Ed and he bought Blacks part of Indian Gardens. Before dissolving the partnership, they had rebuilt the cabins, added on and stuccoed them. They rolled the dice to see who got to stay at Indian Gardens and Frank lost so he bought Ed out. Frank operated the rink and cabins until 1948. That year, Frank and Ed again became partners and bought the land from the Thompson brothers and built a grocery store, the one still there.

The skating rink had become very popular and people were coming from Sedona, Flagstaff and the Verde Valley area. A lot of schools had their end of school ditch day there. The year Paul and I were in 8th grade, Sedona had their picnic there. We didn't have far to walk.

The men started work on their store on October 1, 1948 and finished April 15, 1949. In the year 1948-49, we had an especially big snow. The partners quit working during the big snow and sealed up the rink. In 1948 before the store was finished, they put in gas pumps. I know it was Texaco, as I remember the big star on the tall sign.

Other gas stations in the Canyon were at Pendley's Slide Rock Store and Cabins, at Don Hoel's Store and Cabins, and at Pine Flats where Leo Flood had a store.

Ed and Frank built the store by themselves. It has beautiful rockwork on it. Red Hedges mixed mud for them. After finishing the store, they put in the trailer park, mostly along the creek. They poured 75 slabs for trailers in about 1952 or 53. The men added onto the rink on the West Side. The skating area was over 50 feet long and the whole area about 70feet long and 40 feet wide. The north end of the rink, next to the store, was where you got skates and there were pinball games. The west side had a fireplace and pool tables. Rest rooms were on the west side.

They built a rock storage room next to the mountain north of the store. Frank and sons, Wesley and Franklin Delano, known as "Skikee", lived in a cabin behind the store. Ed Black and wife Frances built a nice house to the south of the rink on a hill. They had daughter Helen and son Lewis known as "Rusty". Helen married Arley Jack Brewer. Originally, there were bathrooms and showers behind the store for cabins and trailers.

Frank married Dora Parker, widow of Denver Parker. She had daughters Patsy, Ruth, Jeannie and Fay, and sons Larry, Mike and Marshall. The men were partners from 1948 until 1958 when they dissolved the partnership and cut the property in two. Ed took the rink and the big part of the property south and east. Frank took the store and

Turning Back the Pages of Time II

most of the cabins, Bacon Rind Park and the area where the spring came out. While still partners, Frank and family ran the store. Ed and Rusty were at the rink. Ed was right out with the skaters holding up signs telling them what to do. There was a jukebox. One of my favorites was the "Skaters Waltz".

Sometime in the 70's, Ed Black sold his part to the Forest Service. For a time he and Frances lived at the old Thompson house before it was also sold and all buildings but the spring house torn down. The rink was bought by a Cottonwood business and is still in Cottonwood.

There was a restaurant in Jackson's Store. In the 60's Jackson's turned it into a liquor store. Not long after the restaurant opened, I met my future sister-in-law, Geraldine Kipina, when Fred introduced Gerry to me there.

In the summer of 1958, I worked in the restaurant for a woman named Mary for a few weeks.

Frank had a cold box, and they cut and wrapped meat for you. They also had long rolls of cheese and bologna. By the door, they had post cards, magazines, comics and books. I bought several books for 25 or 50 cents.

For several years, people came from Sedona to shop, but later in years it was tourists and locals. Frank never wanted to be anything but a storekeeper. He liked people and they liked him. I remember his big smile and how he whistled in the fall when he worked outside gathering leaves. "Skikee" Jackson once had a dog that could climb a slanted tree across from the skating rink.

Lots of romances started at the skating rink. Paul and Cora Mae Boswell from Flagstaff got aquatinted and started dating at the rink. I got my first glimpse of my future husband, Nelson Graves, at the rink. He and a friend were staying with my Uncle Jim Thompson at the Thompson Ranch.

Both Frank and Ed were good friends of the community. Frank told me the spring at Indian Gardens was first used in 1915.

In November 1983 Frank and Wesley decided to sell the store and cabins to William Garland and wife. Dora had bought retirement property on lower Red Rock loop. Wesley had bought property from Jim and Guy Thompson and he and his wife Margaret had a home in Sedona and business property there.

There was at least one dance and several community carnivals at the rink. For at least two years, there was a popular girl contest held. One year Helen Black and Helen Thompson competed. Another year, Gloria Thompson and Charlotte Ruth Thompson were contestants. Also, "Teddy Spencer", Minnie Steele, Diane Watters, Marlynn Lewis and Linda Van Daren. Charlotte Ruth won "Miss Popularity" and was crowned along with attendees.

CHAPTER 4

RED ROCK SCHOOL

Red Rock School was one of the first in the area as it was started in 1891, over 15 years before the Sedona School in 1910. It ran from 1891 until the years of 1945-46, over 50 years. A picture was taken of students attending in the 1890's. They were Erwin Schuerman, Lena Schuerman, Sarah Huckaby, and Nate Huckaby, related to Margaret James Thompson. Also Elizabeth, Clara and Fred Thompson, Ambrosia and Tom Chavez and Henry Schuerman.

An election was held in 1897 and they decided to move the school across the creek. School opened on September 7. The teacher was Elva E. Haskell.

In 1905, another picture was taken of school and children, and the school had roofed low porch, no need for steps. It was unpainted. The teacher appears to be a man. There are eight boys and five girls, likely Fritz and Frieda Schuerman and very likely Albert, Charley and Jim Thompson. The first school was a small cabin that Henry Schuerman, Sr. furnished the land for.

According to Clara Thompson Purtymun, who was five years old in 1891, the first teacher was Miss Minnie Maxwell. The teacher always lived at the Schuerman's ranch house. The cabin was replaced by a more modern wood frame building.

Ellen Graves

The following is information about Red Rock School that Albert Thompson had in a small black book.

In 1898, Nathan Huckaby was clerk of the school board. C.P. Hicks was County Superintendent. Trustees were J.H. Franks and Ambrosio Armijo. Teacher was Miss Charlotte Reed.

In 1898, F. Loma was trustee. School started October 16, 1897. The teacher was Josephine Hance.

On February 12, 1900, Mrs. James was trustee. On March 31, 1900, Maxwell Chavez was a trustee. The teacher was Lily Worst. The teacher got $60 a month.

On March 30, 1901, Ben Miller was trustee. On September 17, 1901, school started and the teacher was Henrietta Dawson. School started on October 12, 1902, and the teacher was Julie Nichols. The next year I have information for is 1911. The teacher was V. Jolly. From 1913-15, the teacher was named Burrough. In 1917 the teacher was Grace Cortez.

From 1920-26, the teacher was Dolly Schuerman, except for 1925 when Alta Owenby taught and again in 1927. In 1928, the teacher was A. Ward. In 1929 the teacher was Carey H. Guthrie.

Turning Back the Pages of Time II

Sherman Loy

Ellen Graves

MRS. FALL, DONKEY AND CHILDREN 1941-42

MRS. ROBBINS, HENRIETTA, MARTHA, SAM, PAUL, CAROL ROBBINS, LOUISE, ELLEN, JAMES, MIKE(dog) 1943-44

MRS. MILLER, MACILLA, HENRIETTA, MARTHA, SAM, LOUISE, JUSTIN, PAUL, JAMES, ELLEN 1942-43

Turning Back the Pages of Time II

MRS. NICKLIN 1944-45

RED ROCK SCHOOL – MRS. JORDAN TEACHER WITH ELLEN, RUTH, HENRIETTA, PAUL, JUSTIN, WALTER JR., JAMES, LENORA 1943-46

At the time Paul and I attended Red Rock School, the fall of 1942 through spring of 1946, the school was a painted white lumber one-room school with a built on rock stage on the back. CCC workers probably built the addition in the 30's. The school had a bell and a raised porch with steps leading up to it. Inside by the door was a place to hang coats and hats and a table for lunches and a water can.

Water came from the company ditch and was pumped by a red hand pump by the nearby Loy home. Heat was provided by a wood stove. The teacher's desk was at the head of the classroom beneath the stage. Some of the trustees provided wood. On cold mornings we drew our desks nearer the stove. The stove was north of teacher's desk and a piano and bookcase were to the south. On the south side, we also had blackboards. There were a lot of windows to the north and two in the stage area on each side.

Sometimes Myron (Budge) Loy built the fires. Before that, Sherman, Fred and other boys did school chores.

Paul and I had a black lunchbox that Mom put milk in a quart fruit jar. Some kids had flat lunch boxes with thermos or sack lunches. Big girls and boys did janitor work. The teacher's house was a two-room building west of the school and outhouses were south of the school along the fence.

At recess, we were relatively free to roam the tree covered hill above the school and the hill behind the teacher's house, including the ditch bank. The last year of school, Walter Jordan and Ellen Thompson fell in.

When Fred was in 8th grade, Mrs. Marian Fall was teacher. That was 1942-43. Cousin Sam Jones, probably Louise Hollaman, Martha Loy, Henrietta Schuerman, Carmen Reyes, a little girl named Julia. Fred, Anita Blaugh and three or four other boys were in 8th grade.

Turning Back the Pages of Time II

School officials wanted more children so Paul and I went while still five to first grade. Next year it was decided we should go to first again with cousin James Jones and Justin Elmer. I am sure I learned something that year but all I remember is that I had to go to the teacher's house and lie on her bed and try and nap in the afternoons and getting my hand spanked. The teacher's pet, "smart" little Julia stuck her tongue out at me and I stuck mine back. The teacher caught me, so I got punished and she went free.

In 1943-44, a woman from Alaska, Mary Lee Davis, whose husband was a government worker, was teacher part of the year. They were allowed to return to Alaska. She gave Dad a copy of "We Are Alaskans" when they left. Two things stick out about that year. Justin's mother and sister-in-law, Dorothy Elmer, helped out the teacher.

We four first graders sat on the stage and the women went around shushing us while the teacher was busy with the older students. I really enjoyed the picnic by the creek under a bluff, and playing there. It was the only time I was there. We went along the old road that used to cross the creek there.

Second grade teacher, Mrs. Virgie Robbins did early territorial teaching in the Prescott area. The name of the story is Virgie Hite Robbins, a teacher in 1902 as told by Virgie Robbins and Catherine Bozard. Mrs. Gussie Miller from Middle Verde took over from Mrs. Davis. Virgie graduated from Tecumpech, Nebraska at age 18. She and her sister, Catherine, came to stay with their Uncle Tom Fitzsimmons. They made friends and joined in the social life. She took her test to become a teacher from School Superintendent, Mr. Jolly. Her first job was in Crown King, 65 miles away in the Bradshaw Mountains. Some area mines nearby were Blue Bell, the Old Tiger and the Lincoln.

The Saturday before school began, Virgie rode her horse, Chip, without escort over a rough trail from Prescott. Miners treated her well, gave her water and directions. The first night, she spent at the Senator Mine. At noon the next day, she ate with Mrs. Goodwin. As night fell, she saw lights from the Lincoln Mine on to the Wild Flower arriving at Crown King at 10. She received a warm welcome from people who were about to search for her.

Virgie lived with Dr. and Mrs. McDonald and got paid $40 for room and board.

School was held in the large Miners' Hall and had 32 pupils, first – eighth, ages 6-16. She got $75 a month. Crown King is 7,000 feet so it was a cold winter. She enjoyed dances and pie suppers. Students liked her and did well when Superintendent Jolly came to test them. There were 400 men and 30 married women with Virgie. She dated mining engineers.

Virgie also taught at Groom Creek, Granit Mountain and Williamson Valley. In 1910, romance found Virgie and she married Bob Robbins

Turning Back the Pages of Time II

of Prescott and Clarkdale. They had 3 sons, Billy, Dick and Tommy, well known in the Prescott area.

She did not teach again until the war years when teachers were scarce and she came to teach at our Red Rock School.

Forty eight years after her first school, Virgie wished all teachers could have as enjoyable and interesting a first school as her first territorial school in 1906. This information about Mrs. Robbins came from Tales of Old Yavapai.

I liked both first grade teachers, but my second grade teacher in 1944-45 was one of the best and most loved teachers I had.

Mrs. Robbins lived in Clarkdale and her husband Bob was a constable there. I don't know where Mrs. Fall lived but on Friday evening and Sunday evening, somebody had to be at the Sedona bus station and take her between there and Red Rock. The year Mrs. Robbins taught, they kept their granddaughter, third grader Carol Ann Robbins, a pretty girl with dark curls. Her family lived in San Francisco and her mother had twin babies to care for. Very likely, the family thought it would be a good experience for her to live in a small town and go to a one-room school. Bob and Virginia Robbins had a friendly black and white longhaired bird dog named Mike. He loved to fetch sticks in the ditch even when icicles formed on the little falls in the company ditch.

SAM AND JAMES JONES WITH ELLEN AND PAUL THOMPSON – READY FOR SCHOOL

PICNIC ANT OAK CREEK WITH MRS ROBBINS

Our end of school picnic was held by the creek to the southwest on the old road that used to cross the creek below the school to a ranch likely where the Jones' family lived when they came from New Mexico. Mrs. Wentworth and helper, who claimed to be related to the famous Dalton's lived there. Two children from Clarkdale and our small cousins from Indian Gardens, Janet, Garnet and Roy Thompson and little Lanora Schuerman were present. Sam and James Jones, Martha Loy, Henrietta Schuerman, Louise Hollamon, Carol Robbins, and Justin, Paul and I were the students.

MRS. NICKLIN, TEACHER LOUISE CLAIRE, JR., MARTHA, HENRIETTA JAMES, ELLEN, JUSTIN & PAUL

In third grade, 1944-45, we had Mrs. Abby Nicklen and Bulldog Booby. She said she got a real booby prize. Her son, Jerry, took her to and from school. During the school year, she had an outside play behind the teacher's house on the hill just at sunset. We wore Indian headbands. After a battle, a warrior died tragically, just as the sun set. Another program was held in the school afterwards. All these ladies stayed in teacher's house.

In the last year of school at Red Rock, Mrs. Ruth Jordan drove down from Sedona bringing daughter F. Ruth Jordan, an 8th grader and Walter Jr., a 5th grade. Once or twice she brought Walter's big truck. The students were Lanore Schuerman, Paul & Ellen Thompson, James Jones, Justin Elmer, Walter Jordan, F. Ruth Jordan, Henrietta Schuerman.

CHILDREN DRESSED AS INDIANS

Red Rock school district number 27 usually had while we lived there, Myron Loy, Henry Schuerman, Albert Thompson or Claire Jones as board members. Three members served each year.

Mrs. Jordan joined in most of our games. We played baseball and lots of games such as run sheep run, anti-over the teacher's house, and Red Rover come over. We also played London Bridge is Falling down, and Gossip. It was a fun one. One player would whisper something in another's ear. At the end it was usually quite different from what it started out. The girls played house in the bushes

Turning Back the Pages of Time II

above the school and all explored. The teacher called us in by a little hand bell; the big bell was seldom rung.

For holidays, artistic kids made colored chalk pictures on our boards. We decorated windows and pictures were made and put up. At Christmas, we strung paper chains around the room and on our Christmas tree. We decorated for Halloween; Thanksgiving, Washington's Birthday, Lincoln's Birthday, Valentine's Day and Easter. Mom always made a new dress for me for Christmas and she did my hair in rag curlers instead of my usual doggy ear braids. All teachers made Christmas special for us. Mrs. Jordan was my other favorite teacher.

Ellen Graves

CHAPTER 5

THIS IS A SHORT CHAPTER MADE UP OF RED ROCK SCHOOL NEWS 1942-43

Among the treasures I saved over the years, I recently came across School News that Teacher Marion Fall and possibly students put together. Brother Fred Schuerman wrote Paul on the front and Fred on the back. Some of writing is blurred and hard to read.

The title has big blue and red title letters. The first page has stick children rolling a hoop, carrying dishes, running and a big pile of scrap iron. In the middle of the second page are trees and kids playing ball and a ship.

Red Rock School News

Red Rock opened with an attendance of ten children. Our teacher was Mrs. Fall. Later in the year Martha Loy left and Wendell Despain came so we still had ten pupils.

On October 30, 1942, our school had a Halloween program. We had a play by the name "The Runaway Pumpkin", which was a puppet performance. After the play we had a dance which many people attended.

One day in November, our teacher received a letter telling our school to collect as much scrap as it could. The scrap was iron, steel, other metals and rubber. One evening, the older boys went to help

Turning Back the Pages of Time II

the farmers collect scrap on their farms. We piled the scrap, about 8 tons, near the road. Some WPA trucks came and got it. We were glad to help our government to win the war. We bought library books with the scrap money.

We had the Christmas program on Friday, December 18th. The play was called "The Great Guest" and Carmen was Conrad the Cobbler. He also had a donkey that a picture was made of children riding and him leading at the school. Conrad was waiting for the great guest, but the only ones that came were a beggar and a little girl. Conrad helped them all. We also had recitations and songs and a Christmas tree. Fred was the Santa Claus. After the program, there was a dance during which cake and sandwiches were served.

"Peace on Earth Good Will to Men".

On Arbor Day, the children brought shovels, hoes and rakes. We cleaned up our school ground.

We built a small wall along the southwestern side of the school, which will help level the playground. We built the wall from the rocks we carried off the school ground. We made two triangles bordered by rocks on either side of the front step. After filling them in with dirt, we planted grass where we hoped to have a small lawn. (Sorry to say the grass didn't do well).

Easter Egg Hunt

We had our Easter egg hunt on April 23. The eggs were hidden at the small green near the mailboxes and everyone had a good time.

On April 30, we have an exhibit and play our closing day, which we were all practicing for last day of school.

On May 14th, the 8th grade will graduate.

A note from Fred's teacher Matty Evans: Mabel, this is Fred's piece. Will you help him learn it? I'll help him here too. Thanks, Matty.

New Christmas Laws

Now why should Christmas be so pokey?
And then when it does come
Before a fellow even knows it
It's over and gone
I mean to try my very best
When I get big and stronger
To see that Christmas hurries more
And stays a great deal longer

CHAPTER 6

MORE RED ROCK SCHOOL AND AREA SCHOOLS

My half- brother, Fred Schuerman, gave me this information.

When Fred was in first grade at Red Rock in 1933-34, he had Matty Evans for teacher. Mrs. Naomi Bunger was his second and third grade teacher. Priscilla Smith who later married Sherman Loy's uncle, was Fred's best and favorite teacher. She taught his 5th and 6th year. Marion P. Fall was his 7th and 8th grade teacher in 1940-43.

Some of the students who went with Fred were Sherman Loy, Jane, Dale and Henrietta Schuerman, Martha Loy, Jay and James Elmer, Bill and Sylver Gaddis, Carmen Reyes and sister Micala, Wayne Gatlin, Anita Blaugh, Simon and Julia Ramez, Sam Jones, Louise Hollamon. When Fred was in 8th grade, Paul and Ellen Thompson started school.

Some of the children who went before Fred were Dora and Ambrocito Chavez, Getha and Dorothy Owenby.

His first year of high school, Fred went to Clarkdale. He and Sherman rode bikes or were taken to the highway and rode to school with teacher Russell Taylor who lived in Oak Creek Canyon. The following year, Fred stayed with Winslow friends. Not getting the special courses he hoped for, he came home at Christmas.

Ellen Graves

The following information I got from Albert Thompson.

In 1919, three families in Oak Creek Canyon petitioned for a school nearer home than Sedona. They raised money by subscription. When they got $100 or so the county decided to build a schoolhouse. It was built on a flat across from Frank Pendley's ranch. District 21 was established and school started In March 1920. The first teacher was Mrs. Agnes McGookin. This school lasted until 1942-43 (I wrote this as a school assignment on November 15, 1951. I got a good grade on it and other school history).

MRS. RUTH JORDAN'S CLASS REUNION 1984

Mrs. Ruth Jordan enjoyed the last year she taught which was at Red Rock 1945-46. In 1981, she thought a reunion with her pupils at Red Rock

Turning Back the Pages of Time II

would be enjoyable for all. She and eighth grade pupil, Henrietta Schuerman Satran, made plans to meet at the old Schuerman ranch where Henrietta and Mirc Satran lived. Her grandparents and parents, Henry and Jewel, had lived there. First grader Lanora Schuerman Clemson and husband, Lee, lived on part of the ranch.

We met on a beautiful fall day at 11A.M. on October 17, 1981. The teacher was Ruth Jordan, 8th graders F. Ruth Jordan, Henrietta Schuerman, 5th grader Walter Jordan Jr., 4th graders Justin Elmer, James Jones, Paul and Ellen Thompson, and first grader Lanora Schuerman. Eight in all attended.

We brought potluck and Henrietta presented our teacher with a lovely yellow orchid. Pictures were taken and Ruthie read a poem she wrote in 1972 called "Red Rock, Mother and Me". A reporter from the Red Rock News was present.

We had a gab session, and Mrs. Jordan remembered her funniest moment. On Halloween, Ruthie and Henrietta dressed as a cow, with cow head, hide and tail and burlap legs. Ruth was the head and Henrietta the tail, and I doubt she could see well. As the girls moved stomping and mooing, a little dog, probably Loy's dog "Wilky", kept grabbing the cows tail. Henrietta kept kicking at him and a great time was had by all. The teacher's house was made into a fun house, all dark and spooky with cobwebs and ghosts. I remember the worms (spaghetti).

The teacher's house was used once a week when the Jordan's friends, Pastor and Mrs. Buhler, came from Cottonwood to teach. He taught shop and she taught music. She also played the piano for our Christmas program. He had a magnificent voice and at Christmas, he and Walter and George Jordan sang for part of the program.

During the year, we made a field trip up to see Walter Jordan's pumping system and he showed us through it. It was located at the creek below "The Point". Ruth said she felt smarter than the rest of us because it was old stuff to her. All the machinery and pipes impressed me.

About a week after school let out, Mrs. Jordan arranged another field trip. This time, we went at night to Flagstaff to Lowell Observatory. Mr. and Mrs. Jordan, and possibly Uncle Claire Jones went. Brother Fred took Mom, Paul and me. Because I feared deep dark holes and was afraid I would fall, I did not enjoy looking through the telescope very much. Later I got to go to Palomar Observatory in California with Nelson during his Navy days. We went during the day and I was very impressed.

At the reunion, Walter remembered he and other boys talked of ditching school. When the teacher heard, she said "Go ahead" and all ditched on an exploring trip to the creek.

The last day of the school program, we supposedly held a reunion after many years. I was an old maid school teacher who kept house for my pilot brother. At our gathering I asked Henrietta what she planned to be and she had not known and still didn't. Ruth said she never planned to be anything but a teacher. (Henrietta upholstered furniture and she helped her husband when he piloted his plane). During floods, they spotted victims and rescued people. I became a wife and mother and Paul worked for the Park Service.

We went to the site of Red Rock School. Nothing but the rock stage remained and the teacher's house. Now both are gone. The area was grown up with cactus and small trees.

Pictures were made as much like the original as possible. Only Justin Elmer and wife Carol of Cornville weren't there.

While all were talking, my Mom Mabel reminded Mrs. Jordan of the band she got together. I played cymbals, somebody a triangle and we had bells. Henrietta played xylophone, and we had similar instruments. We made wonderful music!

James and Madeline Jones came from Red Rock. Paul and Cora Mae left at 4 A.M. from Organ Pipe Cactus National Monument to come up. Ellen Thompson Graves and husband Nelson and most of their seven children came from the canyon. Oldest son, Jack, brought Grandmother Mabel. Walter Jordan Jr. brought his Mother and Dad from Sedona. Ruth Jordan Jackson and her son came from the Phoenix area. Lanora and Lee Clemson's two sons and little Laura Lee came from Red Rock.

We pupils were lucky to have a teacher with innovative ideas for our education and enjoyment.

I used information from Dad's diary.

On September 15, we went to a school birthday party for Henrietta and it was for him too. Mrs. Jordan believed in fun and knew Henrietta was a good sport. They had her look through a coat sleeve to see stars and poured water in it. Then they blind folded her and got her on a table. They told her they would lift her so she could touch the ceiling. Instead, they took a board and gently touched her head with it.

Mrs. Jordan had a Valentine party at night and all enjoyed it.

In a Halloween play, Henrietta was a witch. We all flew away on broomsticks.

At Christmas, I was a little girl who was supposed to hang my stocking. Mrs. Jordan had to help me.

On Saturday, May 10, we took in a last day of school program and Paul and I finished 4th grade.

On Monday, May 12, Mrs. Jordan gave a surprise birthday party for Paul and me. Everybody was supposed to gather and clean the school we thought. Paul and I received a book from Mrs. Jordan. Mine was Alice in Wonderland. We had cake and several people gave us cards and it was one of our nicest birthdays. The folks always had family parties or picnics for us. The only other special birthday was my 70th held at Montezuma

Turning Back the Pages of Time II

Well by my girls Ruth, Judy and Laurel and family and friends came.

Poem Ruth Jordan Jackson Van Eppes wrote for her Mother.

Mother, Red Rock and Me.

Memories of so great a year are wrapped around you, Mother. A year of learning, exploring and fun, with variety and action for everyone.

A cow skull was found for science one day Ah ha! A Halloween costume, no other way Thus Henrietta and I roamed, kicked and as many at the party we mooed actively schooed.

Music, art and woodworking, too

After math and reading we could do

With only you and four grades in the room

We learned how to help, to share and wait our turn.

As I look back over the time I spent trying to discover what life really meant, there is one outstanding thing in my mind, the year at Red Rock, tops all I find.

I thank you, Mother for all you did in that one room school with eight kids. I thank the other seven of you too. For friendships that still remain true.

Your daughter   Ruth 5/12/71

CHAPTER 7

EXCERPTS FROM LETTERS

Earlier in this book, I wrote about Dad's early day trips in Northern Utah. While my husband and I were living in St. George, Utah, we took a trip into Northeast Utah. Dad wrote me at St. George; "August 1, 1969 Munds Creek, AZ

Dear Ellen and All,

It seems you had a very interesting trip. I saw a little of that country 42 years ago in 1927. Going North on present 89, we, Brother Greene and I, turned off at either Salina or Richfield. We crossed the Sevier River and camped for the night. Next morning we went east up the mountain. It was the 7th or 8th of June. Where we crossed the mountain, it wasn't near as high as you were. No Aspens or Pines, just Cedar and Pinions. There was a lot of snow in patches and drifts that was melting and creeks running everywhere. On the East Side we went through Ferron and Emory County and up to Price. When we left Uinta Basin, September 1927 it had rained so much the main road to Price was closed by mudslides. We crossed Duchesne River at Myton and took what they called the 9-mile road. I don't know where the 9 miles came in for it was a long way across. I climbed an awfully high mountain and went over a divide and thought I was over it, but went down a long hill to Minnie Maud Creek. We thought the road went up so we went up it. After going miles, I came to a washed out bridge. It was a small creek so I drove in and got stuck in the mud. It was late evening and it began to rain. A man came along on horseback and he said there was a team and wagon behind. They were a road crew on the way to camp. When the team pulled me out, the driver said there was a sheep ranch further on with a barn we could camp in. The rain didn't last but there was a lot of lightening among the big firs. The man at the sheep ranch was so happy to have company, he would not let us sleep in the barn, but had us bring our bed into the house, and fed us supper and breakfast. The next day, we climbed several miles more and went over the top. We hit the main road at Wellington, south end of Price and headed for Green River."

While living in St. George, Nelson worked for the Arizona Highway Department, when they were putting the California to Canada freeway through the Arizona Strip. We explored a lot of Utah.

When we moved to Munds Canyon, Dad got blackberry plants from Uncle Ab Purtymun. Every year, they picked a lot of crates and sold locally and in Flagstaff. This is what he wrote in his letter. "We finally got the berries picked. About 74 crates. We got word today Elmer Purtymun died, and is to be buried in Grasshopper Cemetery. Oh yes, my cousin Barbara LeMay died a week ago, Dave James' daughter. I only have two cousins left, Barbara's sister Ollie Markas and Pearl Carlson of Oakland. I expect Nelson is getting the benefit of summer heat.

Mom wrote me on November 17, 1967 "Hello People, guess we did okay at the fair. We won't know until we get the check in December. (The folks always took a lot of entries to the Coconino Fair and the State Fair.) Dad said Coconino Fair paid taxes and the State Fair bought Christmas gifts. Got your nice letter Sis.

Paul Jones stopped to see us. (He was a cousin raised on Blue River). He and his wife stayed an hour. I had not seen him since 1933. I had about decided who he was when he told me. He wasn't married then and now has grandkids, wears glasses, has a little mustache and is heavier. He has two *sons, both over six feet tall, and Paul is six feet. Paul is crazy as ever, told Pop he had a blue ribbon for me when he went out and didn't tell his name. Fort Verde Days were good this year. We played for the pioneers again. We took Mrs. Kurtz and Myrtle Smith down. Aunt Clara Purtymun got lost from Uncle Charley Thompson and returned with us. Pop saw a lot of people he knew.*

Fred got us another big load of wood and I got a pickup load of driftwood out of Munds Creek. Hope we have enough for winter.

Love Always Mom."

Another School Reunion

Christmas of 1914, the teacher at the Sedona School was Edith Lamport Croxen and she had a program. Fifty-two years later, the Sedona Westerners had a reunion for Edith Croxen and her husband, Fred. As many of her former pupils as possible gathered at the Sedona School on Brewer Road on December 26, 1966. In a letter, Albert Thompson told about it. The Croxon's made it from Tucson. I managed to get together some of the pupils plus Iva and Charley Smith who had Mrs. Croxon in 1915. There was Iva Van Deren Fairchild, Perry Van Deren, Mary Farley Hancock,

Ellen Graves

Myrtle Nail Smith, Myrtle Taylor Slaughter, (sister of Zeke Taylor), Venn Derrick and myself.

There was a skit play and Allan Bristow narrated. First a bunch of today's kids were seated on the stage made like a schoolroom. Wilma Dallas was the teacher. Allen read the skit he and I wrote up including the 1914 program, which was in "Those Early Days" book, and I had a copy of it.

There was a flash of light and a curtain came down. When it rose again, Mrs. Croxen was in the teacher's chair, and all her former pupils were in desks. A time machine had brought us to the present. I stood and introduced the teacher and her pupils and told where the rest of the pupils were. I also introduced Doc Dumas' wife, Lenore, who was superintendent that year.

Mabel, Ed Denton and I played a little music and enjoyed revisiting old times until 10:30PM. There was a good crowd. Mrs. Elizabeth Rigby took pictures of Mrs. Croxon and pupils and put them in the Red Rock News. The only one missing was Lynn Derrick, who died about five years ago.

Mrs. Inez Lay wrote this letter to Albert and Mabel Thompson:

Dear Mabel and Albert,

We are going to Casa Grande in the morning and will have to miss the party, which I deeply regret. A thought I would like to pass along about that teacher of long ago. When I think of Edith Lamport, I always think of a red

Turning Back the Pages of Time II

bulky sweater in which she always carried a tatting shuttle in her pocket and did tatting when she had time. It means so much to take time to remember these things that happened when we were young. Hope you have a nice Christmas and hope to see you soon.

Inez Lay

Albert and Mabel did see them soon as they went to Cottonwood to join family and friends in celebrating Joe and Inez Lay's 60th Wedding Anniversary.

Christmas 1914 was a chapter in 'Those Early Days". I thought you might like to hear the rest of the story.

More Letters

I never knew my Grandparents as they died before I was born. We got to know Grandmother Thompson's brother, Dave James, who lived in Cottonwood. Grandpa Jones' half brother, Stephen, came from Texas to visit us and Uncle Claire Jones and family while we lived at Red Rock.

Ellen Graves

MABEL THOMPSON'S UNCLE JIM WEST, TWINS, FRED AND DOG JACK AT RED ROCK

While at Red Rock, Mom's uncle, Jimmy West, visited us. He was a little old man, not much bigger than Paul and me. Later, we saw him again when the family visited Uncle Bill and Aunt Lena West at their ranch on Yarber Wash near Cherry Creek. The nearest town is Dewey.

Bachelor uncle, Jimmy West, had made a ring for mama when she was small, and he took my ring measurement so he could make one for me. I was 13 and had just got out of the 8th grade.

The Wests sometimes came to Red Rock for fresh fruit. After we moved to the canyon, Uncle Bill, Aunt Lena and grandson Rip, about 16, visited us. They spent the night, and Uncle Bill, who loved watermelon, had some for breakfast. He also liked coon tamales. When mama trapped a coon in her corn, she sent him one. They had two girls and three

Turning Back the Pages of Time II

boys and lots of grandchildren who called them "Big Mama and Big Papa".

Uncle Jimmy sent me this letter:

Dewey, Arizona
May 21, 1951

Dear Niece,

Here is a little ring. I hope it will fit your finger. It is all I could think to send you and I made with best wishes and car loads of love.

Always, your Uncle Jimmy West.

He made it from silver coins. It fit and I wore it proudly for many years.

Uncle Bill met Melena Sullivan in Camp Verde, and they were married there August 15, 1905. Uncle Bill and Aunt Lena West's children were Irving, Everett called "Shorty", Alvin, Mary and Dovie. Everett's wife was Laura West.

These are parts of letters our old friend Sue Mercer Burke wrote me from Florida: January 1996

Well Christmas is over and I hope you had a special one. I spent a Christmas on Oak Creek, Red Rock, when I was seven years old with your Jones' family and I had a wonderful time, your Mama was still Mabel Jones being courted by Erwin Schuerman, your Uncle Claire was a handsome fellow courting the girls at Saturday night dances, very lively affairs, I heard.

Ellen Graves

October 1969

Dear Ellen and All,

What good letters you write. It would be great if you found time to write an account of your family's life. What little I know is interesting and seems to me, a clean and wholesome life that turned out admirable citizens for the next generation.

It amazes me that Ruth Woolf Jordan is still up and doing. Here I am an old woman and she was my first teacher aside from Mama who taught me to read, write and some arithmetic. Mama loved you, as she loved your Mama. I wish we knew more about the early days when my Father, Earl Mercer and your Grandfather, Sam Jones, were in the cattle business. Mabel and Claire were children, Ethel was really little, near my age. I thought of Mabel as big sister and Bill as grown. We loved to hear Uncle Sam tell of early days in Texas. Like the time he came face to face with Indians, either Apache or Comanche - lucky they took his tobacco instead of his scalp.

Papa had his encounters with border raiders after his cattle and crazed cowboys who were a menace to Mama more than him. When she was alone except for me, she had her rifle, which she was prepared to use. That cowboy left the country when Papa got home. Next morning he left on a hunting trip but lucky for all he didn't find what he hunted.

A letter from Sam Thompson July 1959 written to me when we lived in National City, California.

Dear Ellen,

If you were here you could get all the blackberries you want for free. I made about fifteen dollars this year.

I caught my limit last time I went fishing and the time before three. A rain today wet the ground about one inch. We got a letter from Aunt Ethel saying they will be up in August.

Fruit trees and garden are fine. We went up the new Black Canyon highway a ways and turned off on a side road for a picnic. Then we went to Bell Rock to hunt arrowheads. We took Paul and Cora Mae back to Red Rock and had supper. Joe can talk a little now. I got Gerry a set of earrings and a skunk pin for her birthday. When you return I will get you a dog pin. They all came from a machine.

The morning my friend Charley Johnson left he said he dreamed that day was the last day of school vacation. He was glad it wasn't so.

I got a new reel for my rod. Now I am thinking about a tackle box. We have a few ripe peaches. I am writing the longest letter I ever wrote before.

Love, your little brother, Sam

Take care of yourself.

Maxine, Fred, Mildred at Montezuma Well 1934

CHAPTER 8

EARLY YEARS OF ALBERT AND MABEL AND FAMILY AT RED ROCK

EARLY PICTURES OF ALBERT'S TWIN BABIES, EARL & PEARL MERCER, TWINS' MABEL, FRED, GWEN McBRIDE

DAD, PAUL AND ME BY PLAY HOUSE

Ellen Graves

FRED, TWINS, OTHER HOUSE, 31 CHEVROLET AND JACK(DOG)

TWINS ON LAWN SPRINKLER

Turning Back the Pages of Time II

FRED'S BIRTHDAY – PAUL, FRED, ELLEN OUTSIDE RED ROCK HOUSE

PAUL, ALBERT, CLAIRE JONES

After Mabel lost her husband, Erwin Schuerman in 1929, her brother Claire Jones helped her on the ranch. After their marriage in 1930, he and Grace Kurtz Jones moved into the upper house at Red Rock, and he was in charge of the ranch. Mabel's

Ellen Graves

Dad and bother, Sam, and Bill moved in with Mabel and Fred until they died.

After Albert and Mabel married on August 4, 1936, they had two hired men. Mike Montgomery, his wife Elizabeth, and girls Maxine, Nathine and Patty. The other hired man was Ray McBride with Laura and daughter Gwendolyn. Ray worked about a year at Red Rock. Brother Claire and Grace and little Sam went to live at and work for Andrew and Jane Baldwin at present day Crescent Moon Ranch. On August 1937, son James joined the family.

About a week before the twins were born, Albert took Mabel to see Dr. Taylor. Dr. Taylor was our doctor. The doctor was called for many reasons and delivered many babies in the Valley area. During his early years, a man sent an urgent message for the doctor to deliver his wife's baby. It was rainy, cold and the Verde River was flooding. Dr. Taylor risked his life swimming his horse across the Verde and arrived late at night very tired. Rest and coffee gave him strength for his coming ordeal. He wasn't able to do a normal delivery. He convinced the man he had to do surgery on the table as he could not get her to his office and small surgery. Mother and baby lived to bless his memory.

Dr. Taylor wasn't sure but the thought he heard two heart beats. It was hard for Mom to sit the weeks before we arrived.

There must have been something special about 1937 for a lot of babies arrived that year in our family. Avis and Charley Thompson's twins,

Turning Back the Pages of Time II

Charles Ruben and Charlotte Ruth arrived in March. Fred Fuentes also was born to Vera and Carl Fuentes. Paul and I were born on May 14th and Don Van Deren to Maggie and Ed in May. In August, James Jones was born. Sometime in 1937, Shirley Russell was born to Dick and Verna, Glenellen Rupe was born to Violet and Bill. In September, Carol was born to Alpha and Guy Thompson and Gloria to Gertrude and Greene Thompson. In all, 12 babies were born, seven first cousins and four second. Later, Paul and I enjoyed playing with them.

The morning of May 14, 1937 was exciting at Albert and Mabel's Red Rock house. Ray McBride and Mike Montgomery went for Dr. Taylor in Cottonwood. When he arrived, Laura and Albert assisted the Doctor in the birth of Paul Roger who arrived about 11AM. Even then a slowpoke, Ellen Elizabeth didn't arrive until near 2PM. Both weighed over 6 lbs. Our folks had picked names for a girl and boy and wanted to keep them. Dad was an admirer of both Will Rogers and singer Jimmy Rogers so he chose that name. Mom named me for all my great grandmothers and four aunts. They were Elizabeth Thompson, Elizabeth James, Elizabeth Jones and Ellen West. The aunts were Elizabeth and Clara Ellen Thompson and Ethel Elizabeth and Ellen McCord Jones. Plus Laura Ellen McBride and Elizabeth Montgomery were present at my birth. I felt honored to be named for those fine women.

In the summer of 1937, my folks got very little sleep. When one baby was diapered and asleep, the other was waking up. Quite a shock for a recent 39 year old bachelor.

In the spring of 1938, Dad made a screened in wood box, Mom called a chicken coop, up on legs and placed it near the house in the front yard. Mom used blankets for warmth and protection, so we could get sun and air on clear cool days. We had a safe play and sleep area while she worked nearby.

Lots of pictures of us were made as babies and later on, especially Christmas and birthdays. During the war one was made of Paul in a Navy suit and later in an Army suit and I had a doll.

PAUL, FRED BY PLAY HOUSE WITH SKINS AND SNOWBALL(DOG)

They told us Paul's first name for me was "Sissy" and I called him "Pobby". When we started walking, Dad built a fence around our lawn and hedge with two gates. One gate was south to our road and the other west from the living room. The old road from Sedona to Red Rock used to go by just west of Erwin's house and from there it went through his ranch and onto forest land up Table Top Mountain now Airport Hill down into Sedona. Long before my time, the road was changed, but in many places we could still see it. The Jones' boys and Paul and I walked to Henry Schuerman's and to Red Rock School on part of it.

When small, Paul got a scratch of some kind, our neighbor Myron "Budge" Loy saw it. He asked what happened. Paul said "I fell in a well and a frog bit me". "Budge said you wouldn't kid a fellow would you?"

About the same time, I tore a hole in my dress. When old friend, Charley Boughton, asked about it, I told him it was my scratch hole. He thought that very funny and often talked about it.

Paul and I have the same first memories. We both remember going to see the only Grandma we ever knew, brother Fred's Grandma Schuerman. We remember going to Henry and Jewel's house and grandma always had Jewel fix bread and jelly sandwiches. One year, she gave Christmas gifts. Mine was a little doll. She died when we were three.

Both of us remember going with family in the old 1931 Chevrolet pickup to visit Mom's Cousin Albert and Janie Jones at Peach Springs. He was an Indian Agent, and they lived by the railroad and Highway 66. I fell in love with trains there. Paul remembered when we all went with Albert and Janie to the newly made Hoover Dam.

Fred was a good big brother and helped care for us. Before we could walk, Mom had a wagon she pulled us about in while doing chores and getting vegetables from the garden.

While we were small, the family had an old white dog named Snowball. When he died, Fred wanted Dad to make a grave six feet deep. Dad thought that a bit much, but dug a nice grave in the sand across Caroll Canyon.

The grownups had plenty of work on the 140-acre ranch. Erwin had planted grapes, so they had to be pruned and tended and picked. In a diary entry of September 18, 1943, Albert wrote we picked grapes until noon and delivered them to the UVX dairy. There were 45 boxes. The Mongeni family ran the dairy and sometimes Mrs. Mongeni gave Paul and me glasses of milk. On September 21st, Mabel and I picked grapes in the afternoon, and I took 22 boxes to Pete Grosseti in Bridgeport.

We also had apples, pears, peaches, cherries, plums, and apricots. The pear trees behind the house had been there several years and were rather big. When the folks raised and sold turkeys, they roosted there at night.

We raised alfalfa, corn, silage, potatoes, sweet potatoes, peanuts, tomatoes, squash and all kinds of other garden truck. The watermelons and other melons were delicious. We had mulberry trees, strawberries, asparagus and one quince. One year, the folks had sugar cane.

They raised, harvested, used for home use, and sold some on the ranch, but most were delivered to various stores or peddled to customers, mostly in Flagstaff.

Mom spent a lot of time canning and making jellies and preserves. Cattle, pigs, chickens, turkeys and Fred's rabbits and bees needed attention. A real chore was keeping water in all the ditches and keeping the water ram running.

EASTER PICNIC, PAUL (SAILOR SUIT); ALBERT, ELLEN & RABBIT MABEL MADE

Besides her household chores, Mom helped with gardening and delivering produce. Before and during the war, Mom sold butter by the pound to Sedona customers. Dad made a wooden mold. Like many of the farmers around, they had a big cream can that they filled and took to the Clarkdale train depot. Harts at Sedona, Pendleys in the Canyon, Leo

ELLEN AND DOLL WITH FRED AND PAUL

Greenough at Spring Creek Ranch and Greenwells at Cornville also had cream cans.

During the war years, the government bought animal skins and bobcats to sell. Diary entry of Albert, Dec 31, 1945. "It has been quite a year but I can't complain, better than average for farmers. We got 8 foxes, 5 coyotes and 5 bobcats -18 in all.)

WETZLE'S CABIN PICK UP, ALBERT, TWINS, JOHN WETZEL AND FRED

CHAPTER 9

WORLD WAR II AT RED ROCK

I have no recollection of the day the Japanese bombed Pearl Harbor, December 7 1941. I was only 4 1/2 years old. Paul told me he and Dad had been tending to the traps to the North, toward Sedona. They met Uncle Claire Jones by the road when he was coming from Sedona, and he gave the shocking unwelcome news.

The war didn't affect me very much since we weren't in a big town or on one of the coasts. No close family was in the armed services, and I was a small child on a farm. It was different for my parents and other grown ups, who realized how serious it was. Having no radio and taking no paper, we asked for news from neighbors or in town. Good friends, Charley and Tina Bouton, had a motor home he made from a truck. They visited and helped on our farm each summer. Two or three times a day they listened to their radio. Many evenings, my folks visited their camp and heard the news. One year, they subscribed to a Phoenix paper for us.

I also have no memory of Germany declaring war on our country. When we went to war, Andrew Baldwin, Claire Jones, Dad and others went to Cottonwood to attend meetings to learn civil defense. Among other things they learned how to shoot a pistol correctly, and the use of a billy club.

Dad was given one, and I was impressed when he brought it home.

Nelson's family lived on the coast of Oregon, around Coos Bay. Up there, they darkened houses and lights on cars at night. His dad worked at a sawmill. There was fear of Japanese submarine attacks. Army men with guns were in the area. A Japanese incineration balloon set fire to forests in the area.

Our own Flagstaff and nearby Belmont Army Depot were very much involved in the war.

Brother, Fred Schuerman, Sherman Loy and other big boys gathered scrap iron and old car parts, other metal and old tires for government use from Red Rock farms. We had three old cars on our ranch. At school the teacher had us exercising to keep fit and learning to knit blocks. We also brought supplies for the servicemen such as razors, combs, toothbrush and paste to be boxed and sent away.

On February 18, 1943 the teacher called after school to discuss changing school time and ration regulations. All of the U.S. was under daylight savings time. There was rationing of tires, gas, butter, meat, sugar, leather shoes and no more nylon's for the ladies. Some of the younger ones painted their legs with makeup.

People from Arizona and nearby states went to California and Washington to work in the shipyards. I believe that Jay Elmer, Sr. of Red Rock and his family worked for a time in California. His wife was Jessie and grown sons, Jay, Jr. and James and Justin.

Turning Back the Pages of Time II

When I first knew them, they still had fog lights on their car.

The following entries I got from Dad's Diary.

January 18, 1943 I fixed an order for new tire allowed me by ration board.

January 21, 1943 we went to Clarkdale and took back empty drum for gas and bought two war bonds for Paul and Ellen.

September 1, 1943 Fair and hot. Budding peach trees. Went to Sedona to sign up for sugar in PM

September 27, 1943 I went to Clarkdale with Brother Greene to get my tire and gas tickets. (Farmers were allowed a little extra gas).

October 25, 1943 I took pears to Jordan's and then went to Clarkdale to try and get shoe ration stamps for Paul.

December 2, 1943 AM Budge Loy came by and spent afternoon. Sherman went to army December 18th.

October 1, 1944 Jack Thompson and bride, Bonnie came home to see Frank and Hilda. He was on furlough.

October 20, 1944 Bob Robbins and wife Virginia, Red Rock schoolteacher, came for pears. He told us the Philippine Islands were invaded.

April 12, 1945 I fixed ground to plant more gardens and spread borax on alfalfa. Mabel, the kids and I went to George Black's for turkey eggs at evening. He told us President Roosevelt died today.

May 7, 1945 we had a hard storm in evening. In the PM, we went to Sedona and up canyon to McBride's. The German war is almost over.

August 15, 1945 we all went to Flagstaff to sell corn and eggs. At evening we went to a dance to celebrate Japanese Victory.

I remember a lot of stores were closed. Mill whistles were blowing, church bells ringing, and people celebrating all over town. We got a few lunch groceries at Pine Flats Chipmunk store and went home.

Paul and I remember the actual day of surrender well. Our friend, Mrs. Bouton, heard the news on the radio and came to tell Mom and me. We met between our barn and their camp. At almost the same time up at Baldwin's, Uncle Claire or Aunt Grace rang the big dinner bell with great joy.

Paul told me Budge Loy's old pickup went by with his horn going "oohga oohga", so Dad said "The war must be over." Dad's diary entry, "Heard the war was over at 4PM.

On November 24, 1945, we all went to Cottonwood and saw Ned Wright. (My Uncle

Turning Back the Pages of Time II

Hugh's Dad.) They gave us a lot of vegetables. Glen and Ed were home from the service.

On September 3, 1946, dad went to Uncle Charlie's in the canyon and both went to Flagstaff. They found nephew Bud Purtymun was home from the Army. Dad visited the Loy's and found Sherman was out of the army. Other local men who were in the war were Ambrosio Chavez, Jr., Tom Pendley, Chester Purtymun, three of the Brewer boys, Fern and known by me as "Sox and Buzz", Roy Kurtz, some of Lee and Della Piper's boys, Aaron Dickinson, Gene Cook.

The only person I know who was killed in the war in our area was Donald Dickins of Big Park.

CHAPTER 10

EVENTS AT RED ROCK AND SAMUEL ALBERT ARRIVES

MABEL AND ALBERT

While going to Clarkdale High School, Fred took manual training and made things for ranch shop and gifts for the family. He made Paul a toy rifle and me a doll cart and toy chest with a key, where I kept my treasures. I never locked it, as I was afraid I would lose the key. In the fall months, Fred was allowed to take off each Friday to help get crops in. While at school one time, somebody gave him bees and he brought them home. The following year when Fred went to Winslow and was away from home for the

Turning Back the Pages of Time II

first time, I never missed anyone more than I missed him.

Since Fred was gone that fall, Mom learned to drive the tractor to help Dad on the ranch, one of the few times she ever wore pants.

Sometime in the 1940's, Dad went to Verde Hot Springs with neighbor Albert Blough, as rheumatism was troubling him. They camped out several nights. It was deer season and Dad helped Verde Valley pioneer, and friend, Ben Copple, bring a deer off the high brushy mountain. Copple furnished the horse and in return for his help, Ben gave Dad his choice of a quarter of deer. He took a front quarter, as one of the back ones had been shot up, and he didn't want to take the good one. We all missed him a lot. Mom tended cattle and chickens, and milked, and Fred got in wood and other chores. Dad felt better from the trip.

In 1945, Paul lost the end of his finger in long handled pruning shears. The Russell's were visiting and Burrell took Dad and Paul to the Clarkdale Company doctor. Dad said he had tiny dog he spanked with a handkerchief. Paul had to lose a day from school, his first since starting school at Red Rock.

I will tell about Fritz Schuerman losing a finger and Roy Owenby a little finger. Both men did a lot of cowboying.

I don't know how Fritz lost his finger, but he pickled it in brine and left it in Mom's pantry when he moved. Years later Mom found it one day among her jars of canned goods, and slung it over the hill into the bushes.

Roy Owenby lost his finger the year my folks and Fred rented Roy and Lena's place across the creek, and down from us. On May 17, 1945, in the morning, we went to Owenby's and harvested sweet spuds. In the afternoon, Dad helped Roy as he had lost a finger roping a cow at Dry Creek on Monday the 14th. Later Dad took Roy to the doctor.

A major accident for Ellen was when Dad and I got in a wreck at the Banjo Bill Campground in Oak Creek Canyon. Not having seat belts then, I went through the windshield and cut my cheek and throat lengthwise. Sedona Ranger, Merle Olson, came by and took Dad and me to Cottonwood Hospital, where Dr. Carlson did a fine job fixing me up. I was disappointed I could not get my two Mexican dolls from Sally Black's Curio shop in Grasshopper Flats. It happened on August 3, 1946 after Dad and I had been peddling in Flagstaff.

The next day, I did get my dolls and a pretty decorated dish Sally gave me when Mom came to see me. Angela, a wonderful nurse's aide from Clarkdale named my dolls for herself and she said her boyfriend.

Sally Black had a lot of fine things made by Mexicans from Mexico in her shop. Paul and I each had a piggy bank from there, and his looked like a real pig.

Turning Back the Pages of Time II

Our old Chevrolet pickup was towed to Guy and Jim Thompson's at Indian Gardens. Guy and Fred worked on it and got it so it could be driven. Guy took Dad to see the law and Uncle Greene took Mom to see me and on Sunday brought me to McBride's. The pickup never was as good as before, so later the folks sold it and bought an International from Russell's.

In September we got Burrell Russell's International truck for $500 and in October sold the old pickup to Chester Michael in Cottonwood for $150.

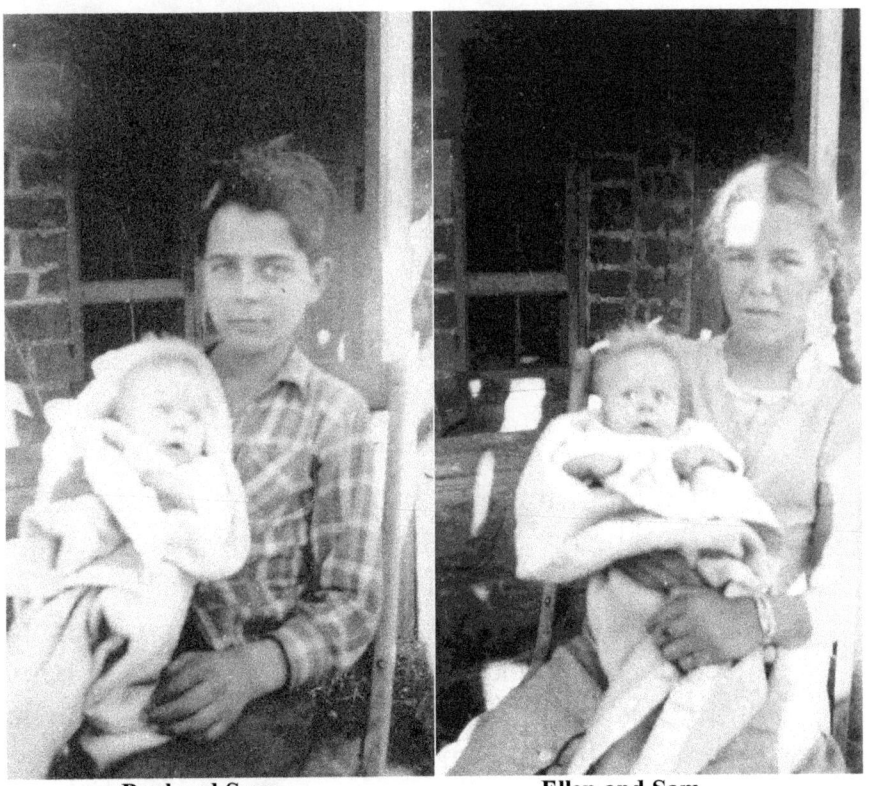

Paul and Sam   Ellen and Sam

Ellen Graves

A big day in our life was when Samuel Albert arrived on October 21, 1947. Early in the morning, the folks left for the hospital and Fred got Paul and me ready for school. Mrs. Elmer was taking Justin, Paul, me and Lanora Schuerman and children in the flats to school.

Albert and Sam

Dad and Mom had killed a number of chickens the day before, so after taking her over to the hospital Dad returned and took the chickens to Flagstaff. After school, Paul had a Junior Deputy meeting. Dad picked us up and told us about baby brother Sam. Paul received his badge along with other schoolboys from Deputy Bill Steele Sr.

Turning Back the Pages of Time II

Laura McBride came to help after Sam came home. Later, she told me Dad served her sauerkraut her first meal.

Sam had to have a cast on his leg, and he and Mom stayed in the hospital for a few days. Dad wrote in his diary, "October 21. 1947 extra big day, Samuel Albert, named for Grandpa Jones and Daddy, joined our family to stay." In later entries, he called Sam, Sambo. We all got pictures taken holding him. Before his arrival the ladies gave a shower for Mom at the Red Rock School. Before Christmas, Sam's cast was off and his leg healed.

While in the hospital with Sam or a previous visit Mom said teenager Wayne Barnes was brought in from Camp Verde after a hay baler accident. He lost both legs. His courage inspired the staff and patients and all enjoyed his guitar music.

When anyone had to be in the Cottonwood Hospital, the wonderful head nurse, Mattie Leyel, paid him or her a visit. Mama and I both found her visits to be a great comfort.

CHAPTER 11

INTERESTING WEATHER AND A FOREST FIRE

I will quote Dad's diary often. On September 15, he went to Cottonwood for gas and to take Baldwin's farm hand, Ben Cole, to Bridgeport. In the afternoon, there came a cloud burst in Grasshopper Flats and water came down Carroll Canyon flooding our pumpkins and ruining them and half of our tomatoes. The next day, Dad and Mom dug six boxes of tomatoes out of the mud. A small cutting of hay was ruined too. Our water tank went dry and the ditch across the canyon was washed out. Our water tank was a big cement rock tank above the house. Our ram pumped into it. Dad hoed and irrigated the big field; Lightening set a fire to a tree across the creek. I remember that small fire. While Fred worked in the field by the creek, Paul and I played in the creek. It clouded and looked stormy, so Fred called us in from the water, fearing lightening. While we were there, either Fred or Paul looked across the creek on the hill and saw a cedar on fire. No trees were near so we knew there was no danger of it spreading. My first little fire impressed me.

On August 9, 1944, it was cloudy and hot and to quote Dad, "a hell of a rain came in the afternoon. Dad and Mom had been to the Owenby place on the tractor and on the way home, it rained very hard. Dad said it was like buckets of water were pouring down and the motor of the tractor drowned out very

Turning Back the Pages of Time II

near Red Rock Crossing. Mom and Dad walked home and he had to help her through deep water in Carroll Canyon and the creek bottom below the ditch. Fred, Mr. Bouton and the kids were in the truck and got caught on the other side of Carroll Canyon. Mrs. Bouton was concerned that cows had got trapped in the pasture under the hill and also about us.

I remember the day very well. It was not an ordinary storm. It was like a tropical storm in later years when Nelson, Ben and I were leaving British Honduras for Mexico and home.

That morning, Paul and I had gone with the men up to the Chavez place to either work on our dam in the creek or on the ditch that headed below Mr. Chavez' farm and went to Baldwin's ranch and on to ours. We kids played, and we all ate lunch. When it began to rain, Fred sent Paul and I to the truck near the road. After it poured, I got scared, and we wondered when they would come. Finally, two very wet men ran to the truck and got in. Before we saw Carroll Canyon, we strongly suspected we couldn't cross as it was a long time before a bridge was built. The rain had stopped by then, so we all got out and walked south along the hillside toward Oak Creek.

When we got to where the canyon spread out and the water wasn't so deep, near the campground, we stopped. The men talked it over and decided it could be crossed. I believe Fred crossed over and upon returning took Paul over to some Sycamore trees. Mr. Bouton carried me. The water was waist deep on them. It wasn't as deep in the water not flowing into Oak Creek so holding the men's hands; we made it across the ditch to our happy parents. Even knowing we were in good hands they were glad to see us. We went up near the upper house to see the impressive flood.

The next day, the men fixed fences and got the tractor and truck home. Mrs. Bouton and Mom salvaged what they could from the garden. That afternoon, Dad and Fred worked on the big ditch and the Bouton's and Dad salvaged what corn they could. Fred went to Jones at Baldwin's place and got a Fresno to try and uncover alfalfa. He got the big boulders out of it.

On September 5th, Fred worked for Roy Owenby. That day, the county crew did work on Carroll Canyon where the flood washed the road out. They had to dig out across the canyon and muck out a lot of mud. Next spring they put a dike in Carroll Canyon and made a drag to level our field that had flooded.

All summer days weren't wet. On September 2nd, Dad recorded the weather as damn hot 105°. He irrigated until noon and we went to Indian Gardens to cool off. Notice that was in September. It wasn't always that hot in the summer months, but I remember that hot weather in May before school let out and again in September. Off went my socks and shoes as soon as I got home. On a July 24, Dad took Fred and Sherman to a bee cave near the Chavez Ranch, and it was very hot and everybody was talking about the heat,

Turning Back the Pages of Time II

After floods and heat, how about a snowstorm? On November 12, 1944 it snowed from 10 A.M. with hurricane wind. We all went to Williams to visit Uncle Greene and Aunt Gertrude and the kids. A bad snowstorm came up so Uncle Greene let us leave the truck and go home in his car. It was dark before we got home. After getting on Highway 66, we had no trouble until the long hill going from Bellemont to Flagstaff. We came to a line of cars stopped that could not get up the hill. Several men were out pushing cars to get them going and up the hill. Fred and Dad helped two or three, until our turn, and we had no more trouble. There was deep snow on the mountain, but we expected much less in the canyon and very little at Red Rock. At home, it was about a foot deep and limbs had broken on two of our shade trees.

After taking us to school next day, Dad returned Greene's car to the Williams' highway camp, got our truck and was home by 4pm. In the deep snow, there were shocks of fodder that were blown down by the wind.

January 1943 was the coldest night of the season. Our water tank went dry and the water froze from the ram to the house and Dad had to work on them until noon.

On July 31, 1946, it was hot and partly cloudy. Dad watered the field all day. About dark, we had a light misty rain. About dark, we saw a rainbow by moonlight.

October 9, 1945 was memorable to me because there was a big meteor shower that night. I was only eight, but I will never be in more awe. When Fred went from the house to sleep in the house across the road, he caught a glimpse of the sky and ran back into the house, and we all came out. Usually at night, you can see possibly one or two falling stars. That night, meteors were streaking in every direction, all across the sky. As long as we watched, for about fifteen minutes, it kept it up. Never since then in over sixty years have I seen a sight like that. It was very impressive, but a little scary for me.

On June 5, 1945, it was so hot and windy in the afternoon. The big fire in Barney Pasture has been burning a few days and has all country smoky. I remember as we came from Sedona to Red Rock, we could see lots of smoke and glowing red flames. My first real fire was kind of scary.

On May 10, 1946, we had bad hailstorm and rained most of day.

Another farmer's enemy was the cold, freezing weather that plagues farmers in the spring, as it freezes the fruit and sometimes other crops. Sometimes, they prevent freezing by running water and smudging. Very often, they lose early fruit. Late bloomers like pears and apples sometime survive.

Turning Back the Pages of Time II

CHAPTER 12

FAMILY FUN AND ENJOYMENT

The folks loved to go to dances and often went to Red Rock and the Sedona School. At least once, they attended a dance at the Falls School across from Pendley's ranch. When Paul and I were small, they went there. We were only three or four, but I recall the music and people dancing. Dad played accordion, somebody guitar and likely the piano. It was likely we were given food, and at our bedtime, Mom tucked us in the pickup seat, and I was lulled to sleep by old time dance music.

I remember a Halloween dance at the Red Rock School and some grownups were in costume. Mom and others made costumes from paper bags. Laura McBride was very inventive, and that year Ray McBride was dressed as a large woman, and very fetching he was too. At a Sedona party one year, Ted McBride came as a monkey.

Some of the men built an outside fire for coffee and the ladies had chicken, ham, sandwiches, salads and desserts. Some of the men had beer or a jug of whiskey, but we had no problems. It was family fun.

Sometimes people danced at home. In February 1949, we went to a party in Avis and Charley Thompson's canyon home where some danced. In my teen years I watched Ted and Gwen McBride do the "jitterbug" at their house.

Ellen Graves

Our family enjoyed hiking, climbing and going to ruins and looking for arrowheads. On March 2, 1943, we all hiked on top of Schuerman Mountain. I remember that as being the longest uphill hike I had ever made. It was over half a mile from our house to its foot. We took a dirt road off Red Rock Road above Henry's house then went across small hills and canyons and then started up. When I got tired and thinking we were on top, Mom said we were only a little over half way! When we did reach the top, it was a big area with fine views. We walked around and looked in several places before going down. If I ever climb it again, it will be to the north near Sedona High School where it is less steep and a shorter climb. In January 1943, we all went toward Sugar Loaf, a road going south from the Verde Valley School, for wood. Mom and we kids looked for bees. Sugar Loaf is a fun exploring area. Sherman and Gene Loy came along while we were there and rode home with us. On Thanksgiving Day, 1944, we took lunch and met a crowd in White Flats. We went to Beaver Head for a quail hunt and picnic. The Easter picnic in April 1945 was a lovely day and we and Guy and Alpha and girls went to Church Rock in Big Park. It was a fun day. Mom and Aunt Alpha hid eggs and Carol, Janet, Paul and I hunted them. We enjoyed playing and the good dinner.

According to Dad, on the last day of the year 1944, Mabel, the little kids and I went to Houdie Baker's house in Grasshopper Flats and climbed to the cave near Gray Mountain. I enjoyed visiting the

Turning Back the Pages of Time II

Baker's and seeing the cave. The Baker's and George Black were two of the few families north of the road in what is now West Sedona. On the birthday outing on May 13, 1943, we had a picnic at Stick Leg Gulch which is at the north end of Wilson Mountain trail. After we had moved to the canyon, in my teen years, Mom, Dad, Sam and I climbed the trail to the top of Wilson Mountain. Gwendolyn McBride was going to college and belonged to a hiking club. She and Laura, the sponsor and several boys and girls decided to make the climb, and Laura asked us to go. Uncle Jim Thompson and Ted McBride came along and brought horses. Mom, Sam and I had never been up, and it proved to be a strenuous but beautiful rewarding climb. It was the only time I was on the upper bench. Many years later, Nelson and I and some of the children climbed to the lower bench.

Laura said the hardest most dangerous hike she and Gwen took with the hiking club was to Rainbow Bridge. The trip in was steep and exciting. She was afraid to look when Gwen, a fearless skillful climber, climbed on the bridge.

On Easter of 1946, we went to the Indian ruin near Joe Hancock ranch in Loy Canyon and had a picnic. When we went to the ruins, vandals had not come and many of the walls were standing that were knocked down later. I enjoyed seeing how they used to live and am glad it is protected now. Pioneer names were on the walls. We visited the Hancock's that day and other times when we explored the area. Sometimes, they gave us grapes.

In September of 1945, Mr. Bouton and we had a picnic near Hancock's. According to Dad, we killed the biggest rattlesnake he ever saw. Mr. Bouton saw it and told Dad it was the biggest snake he ever saw. Fred and Dad came with two forked sticks to hold it down, and we gathered rocks to kill it. It was very strong and flopped back and forth breaking off cactus pads. It was close to six feet and very big around. I never saw a bigger snake either.

On another Easter, we took Mrs. Owenby to a canyon picnic. Going home, the Burrell Russell's and we went to Doc Lays in Big Park. Both he and the Hancock's had a big natural reservoir they caught water in and both had grapes. Doc kept fish in his reservoir. His brother, Dave Lay, also lived in Big Park.

We enjoyed swimming and playing in Oak Creek and Fred went duck hunting. More than once, Fred and cousin Sherman rode bikes to the skating rink at Indian Gardens. When small, Dad took Paul and me, I gave up easy, but Paul learned and enjoyed it. On March 4, Mom and Jewel Schuerman gave a party for Grandma Owenby, a sweet, nice old lady, who lived with son, Tex, across the creek at Roy and Lena's ranch. Roy was working for the Dietrick's across the creek to the south. It was called "The High Low Ranch". Jewel made a cake and both women made lunch. Jewel, the girls, Mom and I walked over across the Footlog Bridge and up the hill. Dad and Paul came later. At

Turning Back the Pages of Time II

night, we sometimes visited them. In summer time, he burned cow chips to keep bugs away.

We always celebrated family birthdays with a home party or picnic. One year, Mom made me a big rag doll. Around Thanksgiving, we visited "Uncle Earl and Aunt Pearl Mercer" in Winslow. We stayed over night and saw a movie, either a Tarzan or a Western. The road to Winslow was Route 66 and we went through Doney Park to Winona. There were a lot of dips in the road that I liked. When Paul was little, he asked why they put Winslow so far away.

MRS. MERCER, SUE, A FRIEND, MABEL, MR. [MERCER & FRED

Mr. Mercer was school custodian. He drove Dad and the boys and I around town and to the airport. We saw a big plane. The Flagstaff airport was small.

We also visited cousins Bill and Violet Rupe and Bob and Glenellen. Bill worked for the railroad and lived near the track. I always liked the big railroad round house that used to be in Winslow. Lee Thompson also worked for the railroad, and he and Gladys lived there. Brother Joe worked for the railroad but lived elsewhere.

In a Winslow store, I found a doll I liked. While Fred occupied me, Mom bought it and I was happy to have it under the Christmas tree.

We always opened our presents on Christmas Eve. When small, Paul and I hung a stocking by our fireplace and in the morning looked to see what we had. At Christmas, we got practical gifts like flannel sheets and PJs and a gown for Mom. Paul got books, games and toys. I always got a new baby doll and once a high chair and bed for them. The folks made a dollhouse for small dolls and Dad made some of the furniture. They bought dolls and furniture. Later, I got a book, a delight for this bookworm. Paul got Huckleberry Finn and Little Shepherd of Kingdom Come. I got Laddie, Anne of Green Gables, Pollyanna Grows Up, Daddy Long Legs, and Mrs. Wiggs of the Cabbage Patch. Fred bought me Mickey Never Fails.

As I grew up, Fred gave me my first grown up purse, a camera, a concho belt, photo album and Paul and I got a leather belt. Mom always fixed fudge and other candy. Dad bought nuts, oranges and hard candy, including ribbon candy. I enjoyed paper dolls.

Once, Paul and I spent a weekend at Uncle Guy and Aunt Alpha's at the old Thompson ranch. That

Turning Back the Pages of Time II

was before they built the rock addition, and we slept on the south porch with Uncle Jim.

The most exciting overnight stay for me was when Paul and I spent the night at Burrell and Virgie's ranch. Paul visited "Windy". Peggy and Cousin Patsy Greenwell had planned a camp out by the creek. They set up a tent, cooked our meal and then came the ghost stories. Patsy knew some good ones. Before long, the older girls had scared themselves and me. They grabbed flashlights, and we went through the fence and fields and to the house to sleep.

One June Paul and I spent from the 21st until the 24th with the McBride's. We not only had the creek to play we had the wonderful virgin trees and rock area below Ray and Laura's house that later became the trailer park. There were several oaks and rocks, large and small, a wonderful jungle or wilderness to play cops and robbers or explore. Ted and Gwen and other cousins and friends played there. It extended from the McBride's garden to present Thompson Road.

I can't begin to tell of boulder moving, tree cutting, stump removing, and backhoe work the McBrides's did before putting in the trailer park.

For a time, Laura ran a restaurant by the highway. Ray and Laura had a brooder and raised their own chickens, many of which she cooked at the cafe. At picnics they often served fried chicken. One picnic at the McBride's, I remember well. The big girls, Gwen, Peggy, and Patsy, thought it would be fun for the little girls to go on a snipe hunt. They provided us with gunnysacks, and we crossed the creek and went where Bee Canyon drains into Oak Creek. Each girl was left by herself. We were told to get a big stick and wait until they drove the birds to us, and see how many we could hit and bag. I suspected nothing so I waited until I heard somebody calling us to dinner. I knew Kenneth Greenwell had been making his delicious homemade ice cream, so I abandoned my sack and thoughts of snipe hunting and made a beeline for picnic goodies. The big girls were put out with me, but that bothered me not at all!

We had a wonderful treat one day in September when we went to Hart's store for groceries. At that time, there was a big open area in front of the store. An old man with his wagon was parked there. The burro that usually pulled his wagon was unhitched. When a big enough audience had gathered, he started his show using the burro and two or three little dogs. He was dressed like an old prospector. The dogs did all kinds of tricks and then the burro performed. Last, the old man acted like both he and his animal lay down and died, and it looked very real. At the close, one of the dogs took a pail in his mouth and walking on his hind legs collected money. The old man had trained his animals well.

Wednesday, June 12, 1943, Fred and Mom took Paul and me to our first circus in Flagstaff at the old Pow Wow and rodeo grounds. They had a big tent for the acts and tents for animals not taking part. We

Turning Back the Pages of Time II

liked the clowns, elephants, horses and high wire performers and got our first cotton candy. The camels were OK, but I was impressed most by my first polar bear. They had blocks of ice, but he looked hot. We both had fun.

A few years later, Dad, Mom, Sam and I attended another Flagstaff circus. It was small, but the acts were good. We got to see a man in an asbestos suit shot from a cannon. Believe me, he checked everything carefully before climbing in. We also saw a very tall contortionist, who did everything but tie himself in a knot, performing inside a barrel.

A lot of Sedona-Verde Valley people will probably remember the never to be forgotten event of Sunday, January 20th probably 1946. We left Red Rock and went to see the Clemenceau smokestack dynamited. We stopped along the road at Gyberg Tank before we got to Cornville turnoff. When it went up, we could see lots of dust and the brick stack falling down. Then we went where it had fallen. Some people got some bricks as souvenirs. There was a crowd there. There is a water tank there now. We got to come back by Montezuma Castle so Paul and I could see it. Mom and Dad had gone up in the Castle when you were still allowed to do so.

Paul and I saw giant cactus for the first time when our family went to Wickenburg to see Uncle Hugh and Aunt Ethel Wright. I was impressed with the cactus. The Wright's had a shoe shop in town and land and trailer seven miles from town where we stayed the night. It was on the hillside on Highway 89 going toward Phoenix. Aunt Ethel had a cat called "Coug". We had Easter dinner with them also shopped in Wickenburg and we were home by 7:30. After Sam was born, the Wright's gave him a belt and cowboy boots.

PAUL, ELLEN AND RAG DOLL SAMANTHA

CHAPTER 13

MORE RED ROCK MEMORIES

Along the ditch below Baldwin's packing shed, there was a small pond. Mom took Paul and me up the ditch so we could go on our first fishing trip at age three. The joy of my first fish is still vivid in my memory. Dad, working at Baldwin's, heard our squeals of joy.

When I grew older, Mom and I fished at a hole across from Henry Schuerman's in Oak Creek, occasionally catching an unwanted turtle. Mom cut the heads off to get our hooks back. No fancy fishing poles for us. She cut a suitable one from the creek bottom and put line, hook, lead and a cork on for me. We sat on the creek bank and fished with worms and grasshoppers for bait.

Of course, Paul and I explored the Red Rock area, as we grew older. In the fall and winter months we went with Dad or Fred when they checked their trap lines. The folks had traps across the creek toward the Verde Valley School, in the cemetery area, north toward Airport Hill and in the hills across Carroll Canyon.

We got "Jack", our small short hair white and brown family dog as a pup from Uncle Greene. He proved to be an excellent trap dog, readily picking up the scent of animals and drag of the traps when we could not see any drag marks or tracks.

I will tell a little about trapping. If a farm animal died, it would be dragged into the hills. They would quickly be eaten by animals and birds and made excellent spots for traps. If there was no carcass to entice animals, trappers had jars of smelly bait. Animal urine was used and also Dad had foul smelling fish scales and gut mixture he sprinkled in the area of well-hidden traps. Also, he had a small broom or broom weed to rid evidence of footprints. Trappers did not anchor traps securely, as an animal would chew a foot off and get away. Before we left Red Rock, Paul and I had our own trap line.

DAD, SKINS AND FRED

Turning Back the Pages of Time II

ELLEN, FRED, PAUL AND THEIR DOG JACK

Late in the afternoon in February 1941, I went with Mom to check traps to the north. We discovered drag marks left by a coyote going up the old road to Sedona. It was nearly dark and started to snow, so we went home. Next morning, in fast falling snow, Dad and Mom, with Jack's help, followed the trail to Table Mountain. The dog led off the mountain on the creek side to the road above Chavez ranch. From there, he pointed to the coyote hung in brush. In the snow, they couldn't have found it without Jack.

Another time, I went with Mom and she didn't have her 22 rifle. A bobcat was in the trap and wasn't hung securely. Mom kept me busy getting rocks to throw. Every time she threw a rock, the cat growled and lunged, and I wanted awfully to run.

She kept at it until she killed him. Mom used her 22 rifle to kill cottontail rabbits as well as animals in traps.

When Fred trapped muskrats in the cattail sloughs of the company ditch, Paul or I waded and the other rode with him in his boat. When Carroll Canyon would flood it left lovely glommy mud in the ditch area for Paul and me to sink in, half way to our knees. Mom likely didn't approve of the mud we got on our clothes or of torn skirts when I followed the boys through fences.

Dad didn't bale the hay. It was brought in on a trailer with a hayrack on it, and pitched from the trailer up through a big barn window, where someone spread it in the barn. We kids liked to play in the hay and the area where the mowing machine, corncrib and corn sheller, etc. were stored. They unloaded the hay from a big corral area. Near the road and corral was the windlass and frame where pigs and cattle were hung to butcher. A big pig-scalding barrel was nearby. A big old orchard spray wagon, no longer used, was toward the shop and house.

Paul had chores and helped a lot on the farm as he grew older. I helped Mom feed, water and gather eggs. Mom fed both baby chicks and turkeys homemade cottage cheese. We loved watching them, as they were cute, and funny, when older, still trying to all get under the mama's hovering wings.

Years before, Mom put a setting of duck eggs under a chicken at Red Rock. All was fine until

Turning Back the Pages of Time II

mama hen's "chicks" got to the ditch and began to swim. The poor squawking biddy was sure her babies would drown. She tore up and down the ditch bank making a great fuss until she found they could climb out with no ill effects.

The whole family helped Mom wash outside. Dad built a fire to heat her water in tubs and got the motor on her gas washing machine going. Even when small, Paul and I hung handkerchiefs, socks, stockings, and our own clothes on the line.

We helped at hay time too. After it had been raked and was dry, Fred or Dad drove the tractor and they and Mom gathered hay from rows and pitched it on the wagon. After it started to get full, Mom, Paul and I became stompers so more could be put on. Once, there was some excitement when a snake got pitched to us, until Mom forked it back. She used a pitchfork to position the hay.

After we moved to Munds Creek in 1948, the family was helping Fred with hay at Red Rock. Paul wasn't there so they had me driving the tractor. Sorry to say, I was the "jerk" at the wheel and my stops were sudden.

When very small, Paul and I had our bath in a small tub by the fireplace. How hot our side next to the fire got. Sometimes, Mom popped corn in a special popper in the fireplace. Wintertime was read aloud time and storytelling time. Paul and I liked the bear stories Dad sometimes sang and a favorite was "The Preacher and the Bear".

We weren't afraid of ghosts at the nearby cemetery. We knew family and friends were buried there. Dad and Fred helped dig graves and Mom and Fred cut weeds and mesquite brush and filled in graves.

We had a big Catalpa tree in front of the house and canteens and water bags were kept wet and hanging there for a cool drink. We had a gunnysack framed box, kept wet, across the road in the shade to keep butter and milk cool.

The folks raised cantaloupes and watermelons. Sometimes, a watermelon was brought in to eat. One time Ray and Laura McBride and kids and Grandpa McBride and Bud Purtymun's wife came down. Mom and the women had a picnic lunch. On the way down, Grandpa sat in Laura's pie. Dad brought in a watermelon. Minnie decided it would be fun to put melon on Grandpa's bald head. He quickly arose from his chair and promptly proceeded to thoroughly wash her face in watermelon. Dad said he never laughed so hard in his life. Both were good sports and soon got cleaned up with no bad feelings.

For my birthday one year, Mom made a big stuffed doll with embroidered face and sewed my blond hair on her. I called her Samantha Jane. The following Christmas, she had a pattern for a lovely big Rosy Red Head, but no yarn, so she used a cow tail, and along with natural curl used a curling iron. Not having enough cotton for the body, she used sawdust. Rosy was dressed in a pretty maroon dress, baby sox and blue oilcloth shoes. I combed most of both dolls hair out and mothered and stained them until they became wobbly headed, but restored them the best I could and gave them to the Sedona Heritage Museum. They are in the Jordan cabin. I also gave Paul and my ABC numbers table to the Museum.

ELLEN THOMPSON AND ROSIE

On a cold snowy day, Fred went to the island for some reason and I tagged along. We had to cross a log and it was slick, so I fell in, on the way back. Big brother fished me out and quickly carried me home to dry out and get warm.

Our parents had a cream separator. Each day, Mom had to wash and scald it after use. I loved milk and was there with a cup for the first milk from the separator. I have already told how the folks sold

FRED, PAUL & ELLEN PLAYING DRESSUP

cream and butter. The folks also sold a lot of eggs at Red Rock and Munds Creek. Being fresh, they could be kept in cans in a cool place for several days without refrigeration. At Red Rock, Dad candled eggs before putting them in cartons and sold two or three dozen at a time.

For a short time, Paul had a horse. Mr. Carl Brown and his wife, Daphne, fine neighbors, bought Roy Owenby's ranch. They had a ten-year-old mare named "Daisy" that he gave Paul. I don't know how his rides went. On my one ride, I had a wonderful time until I got to the creek and wanted to go home. Daisy also wanted to go home, the old one. I had to lead her all the way back. When Dad rode her, she knew who was boss.

After we moved to the canyon, a friend of Fred and Paul's let us ride horses with him, and other

Turning Back the Pages of Time II

people from Fred's ranch to Big Park and back, a trip I enjoyed.

I will tell how Cousin Lawton Russell became my hero. The family went to Russell's lower Oak Creek ranch and all went swimming. I couldn't swim so was in shallow water. I saw Dad in water up to his waist and headed his way. When I got there he had left so I stayed playing in water, until all of a sudden I got near a drop off. I stood teetering up and down on tiptoes underwater and almost into a much deeper hole. Lawton saw my dilemma and rescued me. I was one scared and grateful kid!

CHAPTER 14

R.E.A. POWER COMPANY RACE

All the towns in the Flagstaff, Prescott, Verde Valley area including Sedona had power years ago. Jerome got power in 1909 from Childs Irving Plants in Fossil Creek near Verde Hot Springs. Other Verde Valley towns had power too. Outlying areas with few families had no power. It was costly to put in lines. The Power Company wanted to wait several years before building more lines.

The REA came to the assistance of us farm and ranch families. REA stands for Rural Electric Association and has helped a lot of rural people get electricity in several states. Cousin James Jones told me they had power at Baldwin's ranch from their water wheel, used to generate electricity. The Jordan family in Sedona and Mr. Pendley did the same. Baldwin's also had a telephone as the line came from to Sedona to Red Rock and on south.

Being a kid at Red Rock, I was thrilled by the race between the REA and the Arizona Power Company based in Prescott. When the REA became interested, the Power Company knew they couldn't wait years as they would lose customers.

Mrs. Jane Baldwin was one of the first to want the REA even though she had power already. Big Park, most of Red Rock, Grasshopper Flats, lower Oak Creek, Bridgeport, Oak Creek Canyon and Doney Park farmers north of Flagstaff needed electricity.

Turning Back the Pages of Time II

A few years ago, when Sedona got rid of most of their poles, Laura McBride and I agreed we did not mind the poles and lines. We remembered how happy we were to have electricity after years of kerosene lamps and lanterns, and no refrigerators, irons and other appliances.

Many of our neighbors and friends were staunch power company people. On November 23, 1945, Mrs. Baldwin called to talk about the REA. On January 3, 1946, Fred brought one of the Kittridge boys from Oak Creek Canyon to have Dad sign a REA right of way. On February 2, 1946, Clyde Etter surveyed the line between Henry Schuerman and us for the Power Company. On May 9, 1946, Kittridge came and signed us up for REA. On November 10th, 1946, Albert and Fred went to Elmer Purtymun's in Sedona and met Ed Fuentez there. They came by Lawson's Rainbow End in Grasshopper Flats, and Fred got a job digging holes for power line poles for the REA. On February 16th, Dad saw Ray McBride on REA business. On March 4th, Cleve Keith called in the morning and in the evening, Budge Loy and Otto Hollomond brought a power company man to try and get us to sign up. I remember the man. He was heavy set, had a moustache and smoked cigars.

On May 21, the REA surveyor, Fred Morrison, was here today. On January 3, 1946 the surveyor came to get Fred in the morning and at noon he came to get Dad. That day and the next, Dad helped out in Grasshopper Flats. On June 11, 1946, Clyde

Etter surveyed for the Power Company around our house and told Dad our only chance for power was his company. On June 12, 1945, Dad hoed weeds and George Miller, head of the local REA, a tall young man, came by and said we would have power in days. On June 14th, the REA crew started digging postholes today. The next day, Dad talked REA business with Ray McBride. The Power Company began digging holes at noon. Charley Thompson brought his "cat" (Caterpillar) from near Indian gardens in the morning to work for the REA. On June 16th, we went to Bill Priests after supper to see if he wanted to work for the REA. On June 17 and 18, the Power Company crew dug power pole holes at our place. On the 18th, the power people were digging holes in front of our house. At the same time, the REA was digging behind it. On June 19th, we expected the REA to finish some line and get juice in, but the REA contractor let the Power Company beat us. On June 20th, power company men dug holes by the house and brought a pole and transformer and wire to set up. The next day, the REA contractor left with a small crew to work on the line to Baldwin's.

On June 26th, George Miller and Bob Kittridge came by for Dad at 10am to go to Prescott for the REA court hearing. Dad said George drove so fast and recklessly over Mingus around some of the curves, he got scared. The meeting was in the St. Michael's hotel. Afterward, Dad rode home with Mrs. Baldwin. George Miller and Bob Kittridge went to Phoenix on REA business.

Turning Back the Pages of Time II

GENERATOR AT RED ROCK

On July 3, REA men delivered a portable electric power unit here in the afternoon and it was set up north of the cemetery east of the road. Later, the Power Plant was moved to Oak Creek Canyon at McBride's. Another plant was on Page Springs Road on lower Oak Creek. For about a year, Fred and the power men kept the Red Rock generator going. Then it was moved to Ray McBride's, and they ran both units.

On July 9, George Miller came and offered Dad a job "peddling bull", as he put it, for the REA business. On the 13th, Dad went to Big Park on REA business and ate dinner with Kelly Dickinson. In the evening, he went to Baldwin's on REA business. On July 18 Dad, went to George Black's in Grasshopper Flats to get his sister-in-law, Georgia Hudspeth, to sign a power line easement and took it to Indian Gardens to get postmaster, brother Charley, to notarize it.

The next day, Dad went to lower Oak Creek and called on REA families. He took dinner at Della and Kenneth Greenwell's in Cornville and on to the Cottonwood REA office. On July 25th, Dad and I took corn and eggs to Flagstaff and sold out by 11 A.M., so we ate dinner at Hewett's. In the afternoon, we called on Doney Park farmers on REA business. At one of the farms, there was a little girl about my age, with her hair done up like mine in braids, and fixed with ribbons in "puppy dog ears".

On July 20, Dad and I spent the day around Bridgeport on REA business. I remember a friendly woman on Zalesky Road, possibly a member of the Lee family. She had small braids and admired all my thick hair. On August 1, Dad went to lower Oak Creek on REA business and on to the Cottonwood REA office. On August 13, George Miller came to see Dad about digging more power pole holes. On the 17th, Dad helped Fred dig and shoot two holes. Three days later, Dad helped Fred drill and shoot a power pole hole and Dad did tractor work for the REA. On August 29, REA surveyor, Fred Morrison, called in the evening and wanted Dad to help him scout the survey line down to Dayton's on lower Red Rock road. We all liked Fred Morrison, a nice, friendly man. One day, he left funny books for us to read.

On September 3, Dad went to Cottonwood and collected money for REA ($44.93). On September 4, the REA brought a diesel electric unit here at

Turning Back the Pages of Time II

night. On October 9, the REA men spent all day wiring up their generator and testing their outfit. On October 11, Fred went to Cottonwood for light fixtures and started wiring the house for electricity. October 13, 1947 was our big day. The REA men put electricity in our house at noon, and our house was nice and bright. Later we got a refrigerator, iron, radio and washing machine.

Brother Fred Schuerman said when the Arizona Public Service became our power company it was based in Phoenix instead of Prescott. He also said the REA put power in the Dry Creek Red Rocks area, west of highway 89A. In May of 1946, Mom got her new washing machine in Cottonwood. It cost $111.18.

Russell Taylor was first president of the REA. Later, George Miller and John Redman were managers. Morley Fox was a director. George Miller and Fred Morrison worked for surveyors, Rex Tines and Lofton.

Ernie Smith was one of the crew who brought in poles on the pole truck into Oak Creek Canyon and he was a very good driver.

On September 26, 1949, at a Cottonwood REA meeting, they voted 4 to 30 to make a trade with the Power Company. They got all lower Oak Creek. We got Red Rock and the canyon.

For a time, an electric company from Lakeside came and helped us here. Even now, there are REA lines at Lakeside and Kingman.

On October 10, 1958, at a Cottonwood REA meeting, the majority agreed to sell the REA to the Arizona Power Company. It was a locally owned, locally operated business. Their members elected board of directors from their number. Directors made and controlled policies of the co-operative. The REA served as our banker. We borrowed money from the REA to build our line and we repaid with interest.

Local people organized the co-operative because many could not get electricity from the existing company. We are proud our organization grew from less than nothing to an efficient valuable local enterprise. (This is part of a letter sent out after a bitter campaign to sell our Verde Electric Co-operative left scars in the community. They wanted the friendship and good will of their neighbors. It was signed by: Willis R. Leenhouts, Director; James Barrett, Director; P.J. Morin, Director; R.A. Patterson; Director, J.J. Jackling; Director Charley Simpson; Director; George Kovacovich, Director; S.P. Gimlin, Director.

Joys of Getting Water in all of Red Rock Ditches

It took a lot of work in the spring at Red Rock to get water in all the ditches so fields and orchards could be irrigated. In late March, Dad was concerned the ground was drying fast. He knew it would take at least two or three weeks to get water in all the ditches. On March 31, Henry Schuerman, Dad and Roy Owenby put water in the company ditch and on April 1st, Dad irrigated the island. The next day, it was time to start work on the upper

Turning Back the Pages of Time II

ditch starting at the Chavez Ranch, and do cement work. On April 3, Fred and Dad worked on the pipeline between Chavez and Baldwin's and Dad got tar and cement. On the 6th, they started cement work and on the 13th were done. The next day, they put the pipeline together using tar so that it wouldn't leak.

They had to muck the ditch and replace mashed pipe toward the end where rocks had hit. On the 20th, they plastered cement head of ditch and took out a beaver dam. By the 21st, Dad cleaned the ditch through Baldwin's pasture. The next day, he worked on the dam across Oak Creek hauling brush. Mom helped in afternoon. Then he had to put more brush and rocks in. He was able to get water to Baldwin's where the ground was hard, and he couldn't dig the ditch out, and soaked it up. On the 24th, Fred and Dad mucked the ditch at Baldwin's and shut the water out.

On April 26th, Dad dug a ditch at Baldwin's in the morning and in the afternoon started up a ditch from the lower end burning leaves until he met the water and shut it out until he could fix line. Next day he fixed the pipe on the bluff at Baldwin's in the morning. Mom and Dad worked on the dam in the afternoon. On April 28, he took out a mass of roots, cleared trash and set water on an alfalfa field.

On May 3, Dad cleaned the garden ditch. Later, he cleared trash and patched leaks and all season, they had to take our beaver dams and keep moss out of the ditches. It was so hot and dry it was hard to keep water in the ditches. After showers the screen at the head of the ditch needed to be cleaned. Anytime a flood came in Oak Creek, a lot of work had to be done to once again have water, especially in the high ditch. It took from March 31 until May 3 to get all our ditches in order that year.

ALBERT, TWINS, AND FRED ON A PICNIC TRIP

CHAPTER 15

OUR NEW TRACTOR AND PESKY CALF

At Red Rock, it was a happy day when we got our new Ford Ferguson tractor. Before he got it, Dad used teams of horses and mules, or borrowed a tractor or Baldwin's Cat for farm work. One time, he traded horses with brother, Jim. Unfortunately, our horse died. Another time, our mule was sick, so he borrowed Henry Schuerman's team to finish a cutting of hay. One of the mules was named Queen. Another was Becky. Becky didn't like work and had an annoying habit of running away every chance she got.

For a time, Dad thought the problem was solved when he got his nephew, "Bud" James Purtymun's home made tractor to use. Bud and his brother-in-law, Gene Cook, made the tractor from a Model A car. Dad used it to cultivate a few fields and gave it back. Next, he bought a tractor made from a kit with iron wheels and a Pontiac motor from our Big Park friend, Kelly Dickison. The iron wheels sank in the wet fields.

Burrell Russell's tractor was dependable so we borrowed it in August of 44. To pay for using it, the day before, Dad and Fred drove to Burrell's farm and helped clean his ditch. The next morning, the men went to the farm. Dad drove Burrell's tractor to White Flats and walked back for Fred and the truck. From White Flats, Fred drove the tractor to Red Rock. While still at White Flats, they got a glimpse of the runaway mule. Neighbors told of seeing Becky on Schuerman Mountain and other places. Dad said he didn't care if she never returned.

No wonder Albert was glad when he was finally able to purchase a new tractor from Ersel Garrison in Cottonwood. At that time, Fred got two little plastic tractors, one for Paul and one he set on our fireplace mantel.

Fred liked the tractor a lot. Our old friend, Mr. Bougton, said "if Fred could figure how to use the tractor, he would gladly do any job on the ranch!"

The big day was May 13, 1944. Dad went to Cottonwood, paid $750, and closed the deal. The full price for tractor and cultivator was $1,071.90. Later, when we got the money, a plow and other implements were bought. Since we had to borrow money, the family went to Flagstaff to borrow $300 from Albert Purtymun. He and Aunt Clara lived at the highway camp where he was caretaker. When we got home, we discovered our tractor had been delivered. The next day, Dad began cultivating fields. For a time, the mowing machine had a long hitch or "tongue" and had to be made shorter for the tractor.

After our move, Fred and Dad took turns with the tractor at Red Rock and the Canyon. Several years later, Dad was able to buy a used Ford. After Fred's peach and apple orchards began doing well, he bought a Ford to go along with the Ford Ferguson. Ford and Ferguson were no longer partners.

Turning Back the Pages of Time II

A PESKY CALF

Not just mules and horses caused problems. A missing calf caused a lot of annoyance. One early June day, Dad went to the head of the ditch, up to Chavez Ranch hunting a lost calf. Two days later, he went in the other direction down creek to the Dietrick's place, still looking for the calf. On the 19th, we all went to Grasshopper Flats and hunted for the calf but still didn't find him. The next day, we took eggs to Sedona and went on to visit Aunt Alfa and Uncle Guy at Indian Gardens. On the way home, somebody spotted our lost calf in Otto Hollomond's Grasshopper Flats pasture. Finally, on June 26 Otto brought our wandering calf home.

Chapter 16

RED ROCK AND OUR NEIGHBORS

Few people lived in our community of small farms and ranches at Red Rock and our nearest neighbors to the southwest were Henry and Jewel Schuerman and their girls Henrietta and Lenora. They lived on his parents, Henry, Sr. and Doretta's ranch. Henry, Sr. died in 1920 and his widow lived with her son and family until her death in 1940.

The Old Red Rock Road had gone directly from Erwin Schuerman, Fred's dad's ranch, to the old folks place. When Paul and I and our cousins, Claire, Jr. and James Jones, walked to school, we used the old road to Henry's and then down to his barn. Henry kept turkeys and James would gobble and they would "gobble" back. "Budge" Myron Loy and Frieda (Schuerman) Loy lived on part of her parents' ranch. Their children are Sherman and Martha. Brother Fred is a year younger than his cousin. Martha and Claire, Jr., now called Sam, were in the same grade. Henrietta was a year younger than Martha. Lanora was younger than me but we are still fine friends. I always felt at home at both the Schuerman's and Loys. When Albert Thompson married Mabel, he was the one who moved the Red Rock Road, over by the cemetery, instead of going from Henrey's Ranch to Erwin's.

The Dietricks owned the ranch beyond the Red Rock School. Their son's name was Sid. The ranch was the "Hi Low Ranch". Their lovely house on the

Turning Back the Pages of Time II

bluff above Oak Creek had a fine view of the area. A ranch hand lived below and barns were below that. Another house was not far from the school. For a time, Charley Gaddis owned that place, and he and his family lived there. Leo and Pearl Whitcome and children, Frank Thompson's stepdaughter, lived there once.

The Dietricks sold to the Lyndalls. Roy Owenby was their ranch foreman. Roy and Lena (Helena Schuerman) had two grown daughters, Getha Michels and Dorothy Edwards.

The other ranch on the school road belonged to Otto and Sally Hollomond. Sally was a Sedona school teacher, Elsie Riordan's sister. Otto was from Denmark and had an accent. They raised cattle and often when Otto rode horses, he used work shoes instead of boots. Their ranch was west of and below the school.

On Lower Loop Road, Fritz and Dolly Schuerman had a ranch until he sold it. Son, Dale, was about Fred's age and Jane was a year or two older. Dolly was a school teacher.

The famous aviator, Jack Fry, and Helen Varner Fry, were neighbors on Lower Loop. About half a mile from the highway, Jay and wife, Jesse Elmer, and grown sons Jay, James and Justin, the age of Paul and me, lived there. The Elmers had lived in Oklahoma before they moved here.

Old Alahandro Martinez and his wife had a little house and small garden near Schuerman Mountain

Ellen Graves

and across the road from Loy's field. They owned a donkey. His wife's nephew, Carmen, and niece, Micilla Reyes, stayed with them at times and attended school. Carmen was in Fred's grade. I remember visiting the old folks with Dad before the old man died and was buried at Red Rock.

There was a ranch across the creek on the road that was below the school. A widow, Mrs. Wentworth, and helper, Jack Dalton, lived there. When the Jones family came from New Mexico, that was the ranch belonging to the Chavez's that they moved to.

Other families lived on Lower Loop Road. Ramon and Julia Ramarez's family lived with a man named Vascus near Alahandro Martinez. Wendell Despain's family lived in the area. Wayne Gatlin lived on Hi Low Ranch and Anita Blaugh lived in a house belonging to the Hallomond's. All these children, along with Paul, Claire, Jr., Martha, Henrietta and I, attended school the year Fred was in 8th grade. My first year of school, Wendell Despain was a classmate and again in my last year of school. When I attended Flagstaff College in 1955-56, he was in one of my classes.

Across the creek, to the east of school, was Roy and Lena Owenby's place. The road that used to cross there was the original Red Rock Crossing. The road came from Big Park through Red Rock and on to the Verde Valley. Roy's mother and brother "Tex" Owenby lived there. There were two houses above the creek and a shack Tex lived in. While we lived at Red Rock one year, we rented

Turning Back the Pages of Time II

Roy's farm. When the Owenbys sold the place to Carl and Dafne Brown, Tex and Mrs. Owenby moved to Cottonwood. When Roy and Lena retired, they had a retirement home near the Elmer's.

The Schuerman's had a little cabin above their house and near the road. Mrs. Gertrude Kurtz lived there for a time. She and Mom were good friends. Her granddaughter, Ann Louise Hollomond, lived with her and attended school. She had lovely long dark hair that she wore in curls. After we moved, Jewel's Uncle Cleve and Stella Keith bought land and had a home above the cabin.

Andrew and Jane Baldwin owned the ranch up the creek from us. They bought the place in 1936 from David and Maggy Dumas' heirs. They had a beautiful home, and I believe it was featured in Arizona Highway Magazine the year it was built. Claire Jones was Baldwin ranch's foreman. The Jones' home was above the packing shed. It was a comfortable house with lawn and flowers. A big dinner bell was on a stand near their kitchen. Some of the old pioneer buildings were below the house not far from the packing shed. The Baldwins tore down the Dumas' house when he built the packing shed. At the upper end of the ranch was a cabin for hired help. The waterwheel was on the ditch to the north of the Jones' house. The Baldwin's raised peaches and apples and had cattle. Barns and sheds were above the Jones' house and a silo was nearby. They raised hay.

When Nick Duncan bought the ranch, he named it "Crescent Moon". He and brother, Walter, had lived there as children. Red Rock Crossing was built by Roy Owenby. The Baldwins had nothing to do with it.

At the foot of a steep hill up the creek from the Baldwins were Ambrosio and Appleonia Chavez' ranch. It had belonged to his dad. Their grown children were Ambrosio, Jr. and Dora. I visited them a few times. Whenever we saw him in his pickup, he wore a cowboy hat and smoked a curved pipe.

After we moved, both Henry and Fred sold part of their land increasing Red Rock's population.

At night, when we visited the Jones, I enjoyed seeing the lights of Jerome. I wasn't a good reader yet, so I called on Dad. He got more than enough of the old rabbit gentleman, Uncle Wiggly, and his animal friends and their adventures with the one legged skillary skalery alligator!

Back then, people visited kin and neighbors more often than now. When I was quite small, Red Rock ladies had a sewing circle that met at various houses. Usually, it was held at Jewel Schuerman's house as she was friendly and enjoyed company. Mom sometimes took her mending. Other women knitted, tatted and did other fancy work. Mrs. Dietrick was from Michigan. One day at the end of the meeting, she invited Mom to ride home with her. She asked if she could "ride" Mom home. It was only a short walk home so Mom politely declined. Mom told us about it as it struck her as funny.

Our Red Rock Friends Carl and Dafne Brown

CARL BROWN AND TRACTOR ON HIS RED ROCK RANCH (THE OLD OWENBY RANCH)

The Browns were our friends who bought Roy and Lena Owenby's farm. Carl was a teacher who had planned to teach at the Verde Valley School. Dafne was an artist and they were friends of world-famous Sedona artist, Max Ernst. They were from Boston where his father was a banker. The first time I saw them, they came to a school Christmas program dressed in parkas, snow suits and boots. He had a pet squirrel that sometimes rode on his shoulder when he drove.

After we left Red Rock, somebody shot our faithful family dog, Jack. On one of their visits to our Canyon home in 1951, the Browns brought a cute black and white pup. We all chose names for him and put them in Dad's hat. Mr. Brown's name was Carl so both Carlo and Brownie were included. Sam was happy that his choice of Brownie was the winning name for the pup.

Paul worked for the Browns and Fred worked quite a lot. According to Albert's diary, on October 18, 1948, it rained hard and broke the dam in our spring at Munds Canyon. Our foot bridge and Indian Gardens Bridge stayed in but trash washed onto it. Albert removed the electric pump and motor and carried them above high water. It made the dam higher in our spring.

At Red Rock, Mr. Brown did not fare well. Fred came and told us Carl Brown had lost his new Ford tractor in the flood, and it was almost ruined. He and Fred had parked it near the Owenby ditch at the Crossing and thought it was safe. Fred had left his Dad's pocket watch, and Mr. Brown his wrist watch in the tractor's jockey box. Neither was found. Mr. Brown bought a new watch for Fred.

Fred helped his uncle, Claire Jones, put the dam back in Baldwin's ditch.

If that wasn't enough bad luck, in October 1951, Fred helped Carl Brown get his tractor out of a mud hole in Carroll Canyon.

We had a real treat when the Browns brought us a gallon of pure maple syrup they had brought from Vermont. In exchange, we gave them fresh rhubarb. Mr. Brown was the one who gave Paul Daisy after we moved. She was kept at Fred's and Paul enjoyed riding her.

Turning Back the Pages of Time II

The Browns enjoyed Red Rock and their friends there but Dafne became ill and ended up in Prescott Hospital. They decided to move back East and sold their place to the Lyndalls. He gave a number of tools and other items to Fred and Dad. The Browns asked us over to look at books. He chose three or four books for me, including my first Bible. We all enjoyed <u>The Saga of Andy Burnett</u>, a trapping story by Stewart Edward White. After the Browns moved, Grace Jones corresponded with them until she received the sad news of their death in a car accident.

CHAPTER 17

THE AREA AROUND RED ROCK

Our family knew most of the folks in and around Sedona, Big Park, Grasshopper Flats and the Canyon. Sedona was a village and most of the people lived on farms and ranches. Often on Saturday, we went to Cottonwood for supplies. Usually, we got groceries from Selnas located next to the Rialto Theatre. I would head for the funny book rack, after asking big brother for the loan of a dime. Sad to say, Fred never got a single dime repaid! I enjoyed Donald Duck's many friends, and a little girl who could make herself small and go on great adventures just by reciting a little verse.

Other times, we shopped at Millers, the big store near the railroad in lower Clarkdale. Mom and I enjoyed shopping at the variety 5 & 10 cents store near the malt shop across from the theatre. I believe it was a Sprouse Reitz store. Lena Mongeni of U.V.X. Dairy worked there. Fred's wife, Geraldine, worked at Lillian's Malt Shop before they married. I believe the Trailways bus depot was in that area.

Some of the other businesses I remember on Main Street were Peterson Feed Store, a barber shop and drug store and motel and Ersel Garrison's Garage. At the end of the straight street on the east side was Cottonwood Jail, a bar and bowling alley, restaurant and another grocery store. Beyond the variety store and malt shop was the post office. The park and community building and the Baptist

Turning Back the Pages of Time II

Church were beyond and further along was another motel and Old Cottonwood Hospital. Somewhere in the area of the hospital and across the street was a good Mexican food restaurant.

On really hot days when Paul and I rode to Cottonwood with Dad, I took my shoes off and put my feet up near the open windshield of the pickup. It could be opened or closed. I think at the bottom. How <u>long</u> and <u>hot</u> the road across was. No wonder the road to Jerome in a wagon was so long for my Dad as a kid. In an article he wrote about place names, I learned that early day people called White Flats, White Sage Flat because of all the sage that used to grow there.

In the summer, when at home, I always went barefooted until I was about 15. Once at Red Rock, Paul carried me through grass burrs.

I remember the picnic tables along 89A, all on the east side of the road. One was half way between Rainbows End and Red Rock Road. Another was at the top of Dry Creek Hill by a tree. The third was also near cedar trees about half way across White Flats. Trash barrels were nearby.

I talked to Mary Wyatt and she confirmed my memory of a small highway camp near the head of White Flats on the east. When I was quite small, we went to the camp and a man called "Pop" Green was there.

In Mary's book, <u>A Cowboy's Wife</u>, she said her Dad, Ira Smith, started work for the Arizona

Highway Department in the late summer of 1933. In the fall, the family moved to the White Flats camp. The house had two bedrooms. Her grandpa, Linc Smith, had a trap line in Dry Creek to the west. Mary enjoyed going along to help check his traps.

The Smiths lived there until the late summer of 1935 when they moved to the camp at the head of Oak Creek. Mary told me on the phone that Pop Green took over the camp in White Flats. She said the children of the Green family were Mary Bell, Dewitt, Jerry and Julie Green. After the Smiths moved and the Greens lived there, Mary Smith rode horseback with her cousin Nelly Mae Hart and one of the boys to see Nelly's friend, Mary Bell Green.

When I talked to Fred, he said Mike Montgomery had a tent house at the Westworth place at Red Rock. He got a job for the Highway Department, and the family moved to White Flats. Likely, he took over from Green and was the last person to live there before the camp was moved.

Paul told me the camp was moved in 1940. He said most of the camp was moved to the rim of Oak Creek. A little house was moved across pump house wash. The man who plowed snow lived there for a year or so. His name was Roy Vest. The man in charge of Rim Camp was Van Court. He lived at Call of the Canyon. Some of the highway employees lived in Pendley's cabins.

I will try and record faithfully the following stories Mary Wyatt told me about the area in August of 09.

Turning Back the Pages of Time II

The first road that crossed Dry Creek went just above the present north bridge. A later road was built through present Elmersville and crossed Dry Creek below the present bridges and went up the hill to White Flats. People can still drive on part of that road.

When the first road was being built from Cottonwood to Sedona, Oak Creek Canyon and Flagstaff, a temporary road camp was built in a wide area in a flat just north of Page Springs Road. Not only did Jess and Albert Purtymun work on the road in the Sedona-Oak Creek Canyon, they worked in the area of Cottonwood and White Flats. Uncle Ab and Aunt Clara camped in that temporary camp. The road was finished in 1914.

Mary said a Negro man who had been injured in the Army died and was buried at what came to be called "Nigger Hill" area above the Page Springs Road turn off. The hill going into White Flats was called Negro Hill. Mr. Dumas mentioned the man in his diary. I read a newspaper article Dad wrote about place names and he said the man almost died of thirst, not knowing both Spring Creek and Oak Creek were near. I do not know which is correct.

Mr. Dumas and his crew did a lot of road work in Oak Creek Canyon, from Indian Gardens to Sedona, in Grasshopper Flats, Red Rock, Dry Creek and clear to the Verde River.

Mary told me that when she, Smiley and her parents, Ira and Elsie Smith, lived at Lower Red

Rock, Ira and the women drove to the top of Dry Creek Hill and turned onto a dirt road to the northwest. Ira was showing the women the old Dry Creek Road. Near the top of the hill, Ira spotted a bright object. He went behind a large thick branched cedar tree and told the women to follow him. When they arrived, they saw an old pick stuck in the tree with the tree grown around it. Her dad knew that when early pioneers, the Loys, the Schuerman's, Owenby's, Thompson's and others rested their horses after climbing Dry Creek hill, they would work on the road. The pick belonged to one of those road workers.

Again, while both families lived in Elmersville, Mary and Ira went on a horseback ride. They rode down Deer Pass Ranch Road. There is an old cemetery along the road where several Mexican people are buried. While they were there, a woman from Jerome came to put flowers on some of the graves. One of the wooden grave markers is part of a cedar shaped like a "V". Mary said Sherman Loy had done some work on the cemetery.

Above Dry Creek Bridge, there was a dirt road that if you followed it far enough, came out at the Boyington Pass Road.

Mary told me that Houdi and Stella Mae Baker who lived at Grasshopper Flats had five children. Erma was the oldest and then came Milton, Chesley, Linton and little Stella Ann. Erma, Milton and Stella Ann are still alive.

Turning Back the Pages of Time II

More About the Area

I mentioned the Cottonwood Rialto Theatre. I went to a lot of movies there. The first was when our parents went to an REA meeting. Gwen and Ted McBride and I saw "From Here to Eternity". Nelson and I saw lots of movies there, including the Russian show "War and Peace", a very long show. Nelson used to buy me soft mints and popcorn. After our children were born, Cora Mae took Joe, Paula, Jack, June and I to see "Bambi".

In the summer time, it was fun to go to the Verde Valley Drive in Movie. I usually had a hot dog and big orange. To get there, you turned by the A&W Root Beer stand south of the Dairy Queen. Later, the bypass road was built by the Phoenix Cement Plant south of the drive in. The root beer stand remains but is painted dark and is a restaurant. Sometimes, Nelson and I took his mom and littler brother and sister to the movie. He put an old car seat in the back of the pickup so more people could watch in comfort. Once, he put it on the ground and an attendant came by and asked where his car was.

When Nelson's brother, Dale, got older, he went to stock car races and demolition derbies and took part in them. They were held where the Verde Valley Fair is held now. Our Oak Creek friends and I attended a circus there.

In Flagstaff, I went to the Orpheum Theatre several times and a few times to the drive in, where the East Flagstaff post office is now.

Paul and I went to a few movies at the Clarkdale Theatre.

The lumber store we went to was Verde Valley Lumber Co., a big store in Smelter City. It later burned and a smaller lumber store is there now. Dad bought barrels of gas from the nearby bulk plant owned by Bill Simpson. Tex Barksdale worked there. It was fairly close to the Cottonwood Cemetery.

Three popular nightclubs were all in East Flagstaff. Sequoia, with a big dance floor and small bar was between Arrowhead and Fourth Street. In later years, at Steve's Boulevard "DJs" were popular and The Museum Club has been popular since its beginning in the 1930's.

There was a hardware store in Cottonwood, but Dad preferred Switzers Hardware Store in Flagstaff. The old man was a special friend of his and he always got a calendar from him. His name was Billy Switzer, and Dad bought his saddle from him. Paul said the saddle had writing on it "made by Billy Switzer". Switzer Canyon Road in Flagstaff was likely named for that family.

At Red Rock, our family shopped at J.C. Penny's Jerome store. Mom said in the early days she bought necklaces and her beautiful butterfly pin there for a dollar or less. When we moved, Mom and I bought dresses for about $5 from the Flagstaff Penney's store. When Fred gave us money to buy Christmas dresses, we shipped there. I noticed in the Flagstaff, store the cashier had a system of

Turning Back the Pages of Time II

sending money from below to the upstairs workers and back again.

We also enjoyed shopping at the nearby variety store. As a kid, I bought a <u>Bobbsy Twins</u> book there. Mom and I bought Jack's first birthday gifts there. I gave him a ball and doll he called Charley. He picked it out himself.

Flagstaff had three major grocery stores, Babbits, Safeway and Sour & Hutchinsons on South Beaver. At one time, the owners were Bob Barnes, Bud Cogill and Merle Sour. The store was later called Food Town. It was our favorite store for groceries. Most of that building is now the Beaver Street Brewery and Restaurant. Babbits sold clothing and other items as well as groceries.

There was another theatre in Flagstaff besides the Orpheum. It was the Flagstaff Theatre which was on San Francisco Street. McGaughs newsstand was below it and one of the popular eating places for teens, Busheys, and Moore Drug were north of the theatre. Fronskye Studio was across the street. Knoles Bakery was on Aspen. It was another popular place for teens and adults. Another bakery was on Santa Fe, next to Doc Williams' saddlery.

Many of our shoes, clothes and other items were ordered from mail order catalogues, mainly Sears Roebuck & Montgomery Ward. Oh the joy of pouring over the "wish" book, especially the Christmas issue with all the toys. Then when we got a big brown parcel in the mail, we wondered what was in it. As a teenager, I bought a long blue coat from National Belles & Hess for about $15. Dad ordered a lot of seeds from catalogues. One of them was Rocky Mountain Seed Co.

I have a Montgomery Ward Centennial Christmas Catalogue put out in 1972. Here are some of the items and their prices: For my lady, a handcrafted jewel chest: $19.99, or perhaps a cocktail ring with 8 sapphires for $288. A fake fur hat was $15.50, and French purse $15.00.

For the men, a Timex watch was $30, a 101 piece tool set $74.99. A sports rifle was $12.49, a flight jacket cost $17.

For the little boy, a cowboy suit was $15.91, a farm set $14.99, and a giant tinker toy set $22.95 and a Frontier Town $8.77.

For the girls, there were Barbies, including a 1959 original Barbie. Barbie had a snowmobile for $2.99. There was an original Shirley Temple doll and a 1925 By Lo Baby. "Little miss" would surely enjoy a 90 piece kitchen outfit for only $6.99. A doll house cost $6.66.

I enjoyed the goodies page. Wards deluxe nut mix, 2 lb., 4 oz. was $4.19. Who wants to join me in ordering from Ward's 1971 100th anniversary Christmas catalogue?

Turning Back the Pages of Time II

CHAPTER 18

PEOPLE WE VISITED AT RED ROCK

Besides our canyon kin, we sometimes stopped at Aunt Aris Thompson's parents, Ruben and Vera Hedges. They lived near the Briar Patch Resort on property that belonged to Charley Thompson. All the property in that area once was part of his homestead. A railroad caboose is near where they lived.

When Ruben and Vera moved to Uptown Sedona, I enjoyed my first fireworks display from their house. George Jordan put off the fireworks on the hill where he built the first water tank, and he and Helen had a retirement home. Later, I saw several fireworks at the Possee Grounds.

We visited Aunt Lizzie and Bud and Martha Purtymun. Between their house and 89A was a small cabin. The Purtymun boys and two girls, Mother Grandma Cook lived there for a time. Later, she moved to California to live with her daughters, Ida and Pearl. When we visited Grandma Cook, we met family, including her son, Emory, and his sons, Floyd and Forest Purtymun. One family member had lived in Mexico until their child almost had forgotten English and spoke of a little peen (pin).

We went to see Lizzie's daughter, Iva Nail Purtymun and Elmer and her sister, Maggy Nail Van Deren and Edwin who lived across the highway from the Purtymun's. Elmer and Iva lived at the Red Rock Motel and the Van Derenes were above them on the hill. Sometimes, we sold produce to both women. Iva had a beautiful voice and sang in church and at funerals. Once, Elmer invited us to attend the Sedona Assembly of God Church and afterward served us a chicken dinner. That church stood many years upon the hill above the present Sedona Post Office. Elmer and Iva's children were sons, Ray and Ben and daughter, Mary. The Van Deren's children were Margaret and Don.

We enjoyed stopping by Roe and Myrtle Nail Smith's camp, a short way down from Pine Flats. They had a Sedona home but in the summer enjoyed being near Roe's work. He took care of the camp grounds in the area. Myrtle enjoyed making lovely crocheted articles. She offered to teach me but it looked too hard, so I didn't try. Her sisters, Iva and Maggy, did fancy work and made baby caps, sweaters, booties and blankets. The Smiths had a son, Frank, and daughters, Edith and Catherine, who married Ed Denton and Ronald Bradley.

More About Red Rock

I forgot to tell about the early days at Red Rock in the late 30's when the twins still ate baby food. Much of our shopping was at Hart's store when Black and Jackson ran it. Dad and Ed Black liked to kid around and they got around to talking about the high price of baby food. They wondered if babies were worth all the trouble and expense. Finally, they decided we were. When I got older, I enjoyed looking at postcards and bought a comic

Turning Back the Pages of Time II

one and another with a small fawn and behind it a cub bear. It was titled "A little deer with a bear behind".

One day when Paul and I were in the store, Emory Purtymun came in and wanted to buy us a treat. We asked for soda pop. He said "Ah, you don't want any of that 'belly wash'. I will get you ice cream cones!"

All our teachers through 6th grade read aloud to us after lunch. Mrs. Riordan let us bring animal books, Nancy Drew, the Hardy Boys and Zane Grey, etc. Also through 6th grade, at Christmas time, we drew names to give gifts to. We gave our teachers gifts and often they gave us one. One year at Red Rock, Henrietta Schuerman drew my name and gave me a coat pin shaped like a little girl, with yarn hair.

Paul and I went to the Jerome J.C. Penney's store and got perfume and handkerchiefs for Mrs. Riordan. She gave the kids gifts. Girls got jewelry. Mine was a plastic bucking horse pen. Mrs. Riordan sent a card thanking us and saying what a success the play and program had been. All the school took part and she did much of the work. When we drew names, Wesley Jackson gave me jewelry and I gave a boy candy. When I was in 8th grade, Sybil Richards gave me home made "hankies", and I still have one in my collection.

The girls at Sedona liked Mrs. Riordan because at noon time she would play the piano so we could sing popular songs. "Good Night Irene" was very popular. She taught us the Arizona's state song and we sang "Rag Time Cowboy Joe". During music time, our class sang cowboy and other songs from our green song book. Her ex-husband was Dick Riordan, a member of the Flagstaff family.

CHAPTER 19

OUR LAST YEARS AT RED ROCK

MOM AND UNCLE STEPHEN

In January of 1943, Uncle Stephen Jones delighted us with a visit from Texas. He came by bus and Uncle Claire picked him up at the Hart store. After visiting the Jones, he stayed a while with his niece, Mabel, and family, and a picture was made of her and her uncle. Then Albert took him up to catch his bus home to Texas. He was the only great uncle on the Jones side I ever saw.

In 1943, neither Sedona nor Cottonwood had a bank so we banked in Clarkdale. Later, Cottonwood got a bank, and we used it until finally Sedona got one. One day, we went to our Clarkdale bank and bought groceries in Cottonwood and then visited our friends, Homer and Nettie Land, in Smelter City. Dad brought our ram for Homer to weld on at his nearby shop. After we moved to

Munds Creek, Homer Land built a ram for Dad, Carl, Richard of Sedona Garage made one for Nelson and me.

Usually rams were a great invention costing no money to pump water. A tire pump was used to keep enough air in the air chamber. It took two or three hundred strokes to fill it when empty. Far too many times rams were a trouble and a bother, stopping when you least wanted them to. Usually the problem was solved at home.

Turning Back the Pages of Time II

CHAPTER 20

YEARLY CHORES

MABEL ALBERT AND TWINS
RUSSEL RANCH HOUSE

PAUL AND ELLEN ON
CELLER SMOKE HOUSE

Pig killing was done during cool months. A tall wooden scaffold, made from two poles with parts of a mowing machine to winch animals was used for pigs and cattle to skin and gut them. When pigs were killed, a fire was built and a big barrel full of water was heated. When the temperature was right, the pig was lowered into the large caldron and pulled out when the bristles would be easily removed. The entrails were put into a big tub. The meat was cut into large pieces and brought home.

Then hams, bacon and other pieces were cut, and it was time to make sausage and hogs head cheese and smoked meat. First, it was put in a salt brine to flavor and help preserve.

Dad gathered corn cobs in gunny sacks and took them to the smoke house. It was a room built partly into a dirt bank with dirt over the board roof and a board door. It smelled nice with the burned cobs. The smoke house was below the house by the trail to the company ditches and ram. Dad helped with grinding sausage and making hogs head cheese. We had both in school lunches.

Usually, beef was also killed in the fall. The butchering area was near the pig pen, corral and barns. Dad cut up and pickled some beef in brine. Hamburger was ground, and some was used to make minced meat for pies. Mom canned some. She had a big pressure cooker. Dad helped her with it because it was heavy and she was afraid of it. If the weather was cool, a quarter or two was hung up at night and brought in, wrapped and put in a cool place in the daytime. Once, a bull was killed in warm weather, and we sold some. Mom canned some and part was put in cold storage. Dad cut quite a lot of it in small strips, put it in a brine and peppered and hung to dry for jerky. It was very tasty. You had to carefully remove all fat or after a time, it tasted bad.

One day in May, Henry Schuerman came and asked Dad and Fred to help bale hay. We had no baler so I found the process interesting. For payment, we got hay. The Schuerman's and

Turning Back the Pages of Time II

Thompson's had a picnic that day in the orchard. Johnson grass was a pest in gardens and orchards but made fine cow feed when cut and sacked for milk cows.

Dad bought cottonseed cake for cows and salt blocks for all cattle. Paul and I would break pieces from them and suck them. Nothing was added to the cattle salt Dad bought.

In July, Fred and Mom extracted honey from his bee hives. First, he had taken the combs from the hives and put them in big tubs in the house across the road from the main house. After the honey was put through the extractor, we saved some for home use. The rest was put in different size jars to sell. Pretty labels were put on the jars. Fred put in new combs in the hives. He always left honey for the bees. There was nothing like the taste of that honey that I sampled while still in the tub. People with orchards kept bees to pollinate trees in the spring. Uncle Claire was a bee keeper and when he grew up, his son, James, had bees too.

Our new fruit lugs weren't ready made then. They were bought in Cottonwood and nailed together. Lugs and apple boxes were wooden then.

In August, Fred made apple cider using the old grape and apple press. It was a great treat on hot days. Mom kept it and her grape and tomato juice in our rock pantry built off the porch. She used beer bottles and kept a bottle capper to put the caps on.

The pig pen was kept as clean as possible. In September, Dad cleaned it out and hauled truckloads of gravel to put in it. That fall, grownups hauled three truckloads of corn into the barn, plenty for chicken feed and us.

That fall, we all went to Munds Park to visit the Burrus family and got vegetables. I remember how big the cabbage was. Returning on Schnebly Hill Road, we saw a flock of wild turkeys.

When all the corn was brought in, it was put through the corn sheller or shelled by hand. Some was used to feed chickens and some made into white or yellow hominy. Field corn was ground for corn bread and sweet corn for mush. In later years, the tractor was used to grind corn. In the spring at Red Rock, the corn was planted by a corn planter. In the Canyon, we grew less corn and a shovel was used and corn dropped by hand from a bucket. At Red Rock, when Dad gathered corn from the fields, he borrowed the Baldwin's corn sled. Two people pulled corn off the rows around the field, and it worked like a charm. Sometimes, Mom drove the tractor. We hung popcorn in the barn to dry.

Beans were pulled and put into piles to dry. A pitchfork was used to turn the piles to prevent molding. Next, they were pulled from the vines, shelled and winded to remove trash and then sacked. To wind them, a tarp was put down and beans gradually poured from one container to another during a breeze until clean. Bean vines were used for cow feed, along with corn stalks and hegeri, which we raised and stored in the barn.

Turning Back the Pages of Time II

Cow medicine was kept in the barn near the corn cribs. Mowing machines, other machinery and the corn sheller were also in the barn. In the front were two cow stalls and the hay in between. A big open window to the west was used to put hay in the barn.

When sweet spuds were dug at the Owenby place the year we farmed there, Dad borrowed a middle buster from Lee Piper in Little Horse Park. The Chapel is there now. After the rows were dug, it sure was a chore scratching them from the dirt and picking them up. Paul and I helped. We got 22 gunny sacks and later a lot more. We also raised pumpkins, black-eyed peas and peanuts at Owenbys. After pulling peanuts from the vines, the vines were used as cow feed.

In the spring, sweet potatoes were started in a hot bed and transferred to fields after the weather warmed. That year, over 1,000 plants were put out. We sold some of the sweet potatoes to the Pipers, Rube Hedges, Houdi Baker, the Jordans and grocery stores.

Our family raised chickens and turkeys. During the Thanksgiving and Christmas season, they sold a lot of turkeys. When they were killed, the feathers had to be plucked before they got cold and set. They were hung from a tree, stunned on the head, weights hung in their beaks and throats cut. Dad and Mom started pulling feathers as they flopped. After chopping heads from the chickens, Mom put them in hot water to make the feathers loosen. Both fowl were singed by holding them over the wood stove and burning paper to remove remaining hair.

In November of 1944, Dad walked to Uncle Claire Jones and rode back with a man who was circulating a petition to get daily mail service all winter. We were getting mail three days a week. Our good friend, Joe Lay, was the mail carrier and lived in Cornville. Mrs. Chick was postmaster. Some people thought it funny to have a Lay for mail carrier and a Chick for postmaster. Around Christmas, Dad left gifts of farm produce in our box for the mail carriers he liked.

Our fireplace needed repair so sand was hauled to rebuild the back and patch the cracks on the outside. During the year, the cement water tank on the hill was cleaned and cemented and the grain bins in the barn fixed. Dad also worked on our cattle guard near Red Rock Road. One day, I captured a baby rabbit at the cattle guard. Mom made me take it back and turn it loose as she knew it would probably die.

CHAPTER 21

FARM PROJECTS

In 1946, the men began clearing the land of most of the grape vines in order to plant small peach and apple trees. First, they surveyed 20 acres west of the house. During March, a day was spent terracing the big field near Carroll Canyon so an orchard could be put in. They attended soil conservation meetings and men came and showed how to level correctly. To level required a lot of work. They set out stakes to know where to plant trees and then purchased them and had them delivered at the Clarkdale depot.

Also in 1946, cement was purchased and Dad and Fred excavated for a sump and cemented it. In Flagstaff, they bought a diesel pump and put it in the sump under the hill near Carroll Canyon. I asked Fred what was used to pump water on the hill before the diesel was installed. He said another bigger ram was on the lower ditch near our small garden under the hill. A trail went down to it from above the barn. Perhaps that was true, but Paul said we had a centrifugal pipeline that went from the ditch at the hill where the fence between the Baldwin's and us and across Carroll Canyon and onto our hill. It came out near the upper third house on the ranch. There were fruit trees on either side of the road going to the barn from there.

In the early 1950s, Fred said he put in an electric pump where the diesel had been.

CHAPTER 22

OTHER RED ROCK ACTIVITIES

On May 10th, 1946, it was fun when we shopped for groceries in Sedona to stop at the new movie set on the north side of the highway near Jay Cook's farm and see all the false front buildings. A lot of western movies were partially filmed there. In later years, the Sheriffs' Posse Parade ended in that area, and they had some rodeo events. I watched people square dance on horses there. Another time, Fred took me at night to a western melodrama play there. I especially enjoyed Aunt Gertrude Thompson's part in it.

Before we got power, Dad purchased a good battery radio in Flagstaff. That first night, we sat up until eleven listening to it. Stations from all over came in loud and clear. Oh the joy of Saturday night <u>Grand Ole Opry</u> and the <u>Louisiana Hay</u> Ride from Shreveport, Louisiana. We heard Slim Whitman sing "Little White Dove" from there. We enjoyed Lonny Glosson and his harmonica and other music from Clint, Texas. The tower was in Mexico and the station was 150,000 watts. The most powerful station in the United States was only 50,000. During the week, we enjoyed "Lum & Abner" and there "Jot um Down Store", "Amos & Andy", "Fibber Magee and Molly at Wistful Vista", the Red Skeleton Show and Jack Benny. Paul liked "The Lone Ranger" and Guy Lombardo with "the sweetest music this side of heaven." Mom and I enjoyed the Breakfast Club. On Sunday, we listened to several detective shows. My favorite was "The Shadow."

Often in the morning, we listened to a Phoenix station, probably KOY, and they gave news and played music. I thought Eddy Arnold's song "I Wanta Play House with You" was one of the nicest songs I ever heard. I heard it on that station. We listened to a lot of shows and caught news and weather.

Early radio stations had only three letters. In the west, stations began with K's and in the east W's.

One day in May, we drove up the Creek and got to admire Uncle Guy Thompson's new Dodge car. Fred later bought the old Dodge. Then we drove to Albert and Clara Purtymun's new rock retirement house that his nephew, Elmer Purtymun, built. It replaced the wooden cabin owned by Frank and Hilda Thompson. The Thompsons had sold the place and moved to East Flagstaff. The farm was across the creek from the McBride's, above Indian Gardens. Frank had fruit trees and a farm and Hilda raised flowers. The Purtymuns planted lawn and shade trees besides oaks and more fruit trees and blackberries and had a garden. I think they took most of the oak trees out. Aunt Clara planted a rose garden along their road and wall. She got one from the big rose bush at Tombstone. They had a spring for water and a lovely farm.

In early July, we needed help getting in hay so Dad went to McBride's and got Billy Baker, Walter and Erma's boy, to help. They cut, raked, shocked and hauled some of the hay. By July 3, the big field was cut when Billy's cousin, Lawton Russell, came for him. Billy was a nice looking, well-liked young man, and we enjoyed his stay. Later, he joined the Army and was stationed in Japan. He got to know a Japanese family and learned some Japanese. After returning from the Army, all who knew him were deeply grieved when he was killed in a car accident on Page Springs Road while returning from a Cornville dance. He and brother Herbert and two friends were returning to Williams, their home.

Paul and I started our fifth grade, the first year at Sedona, in early September, 1947. The first week, we went early in the morning and rode the Cottonwood High School bus to Sedona. The bus driver was Gene Cook. After that, Mrs. Elmer drove her big car and took most of Red Rock's grade school and picked up kids in Grasshopper Flats. James Jones continued on the bus as he went to the Cottonwood grade school. I was happy to sleep later but missed the thrill of the bus ride. The next year, we were living in the Canyon and Uncle Charley Thompson drove his big yellow Desoto car and sometimes his power wagon to deliver Canyon kids to grade school.

Our R.E.A. Red Rock generator sometimes failed to work. In January of 1948, it quit running, leaving all the area with no power. That morning, Fred had started in the tractor to get wood and met power company men coming to fix the plant and joined them. It was a cold day, and the tractor sat all day, causing the radiator to freeze, and it couldn't be drained. The next day, since their power at Indian Gardens was also out, Laura McBride and her mother-in-law, Effie Riggins came to see why they had no power. Later, two generators were moved to the McBride's in the canyon. (Fred gave me this information.)

That day, Dad and Fred got the tractor drained and back home but Dad's problems weren't over. The pipe in the chicken yard had frozen and pulled apart and drained the water tank. He got a pipe threader, fixed the pipe, started the ram, patched the pipe with rubber strips and had water again.

When I was small, Dad smoked little sacks of Bull Durham tobacco and rolled his own. The sacks with a bull tag on them, were nice to keep marbles and other treasures. Later, he smoked Prince Albert or Velvet in a can. I am reminded of a singing commercial on a Southern radio station. It went like this: "If your snuff is too strong, get Tubrose, get Tubrose!" I am sure some of you remember Johnny with his beautiful voice calling for Philip Morris.

Things got interesting when a door was left open to Fred's bedroom in the house across the road. A skunk got in, and it was killed there. The odor was so strong and smelly that cedar boughs were partly burned and put in to fumigate and make it more livable. Old timers did the same after a dangerous contagious disease was in a house.

Ellen Graves

On Easter of 1948, the family drove to Windmill Ranch Road, west of White Flats and wound up at the Taylor tank where we ate lunch. The Claire Jones and Henry Schuerman families came by and visited. We returned by Boyington Pass.

On another day, we visited Grandma Owenby and her son, Tex, in Cottonwood where they had moved from Red Rock.

CHAPTER 23

MOVING DAY DRAWS NEAR

Preparations were being made to move from Red Rock to Dad's Canyon homestead. He pulled nails from scrap lumber he got from a movie set at Red Rock Crossing in the summer of 1947. He and Paul took a load of lumber to the new farm to build a chicken house. The movie people had not wanted to pay Fred all they owed but finally paid $75 for the use of the land.

The day they came to make the business arrangements, they arrived in a black "limo", the first I had seen. I went with Dad to the Creek and waded in the rocky crossing. It was later paved. A friendly, cute, teenage actress dressed in jeans, wearing pig tails, joined me in the Creek. The set was built below the Crossing on the red rocks. They used lumber, fake grass and big fake boulders. Paul and I explored the set. Possibly, a building was built there later.

To earn money for our move, Dad pruned for Uncle Claire at Baldwin's. In January of 1948, he had leased the place, later called Crescent Moon Ranch. He also pruned in the Canyon for his brothers, Jim and Guy and pruned at both our ranches. Early in April, Paul and I accompanied him to our canyon home and explored the ranch, especially Munds Creek. On another Saturday, we all went and found a big rock that had to be moved from our road. The men repaired fences. Oak

Ellen Graves

Creek was down from snow flooding and we could cross but our little creek was still high. Our crossing had no cement in it yet. It was fun to wade but needed repairs after the floods. After we moved, my parents, Charley, Albert and Clara Purtymun, the McBride's and other neighbors built a cement dip. Years later, Steve Rhore, the man who bought Purtymun's farm, subdivided it and built the present cattle guard bridge.

Dad cultivated and planted a garden and watered and tended it.

While working there in April, he saw Uncle Ab Purtymun and Ray McBride pouring cement for a new foot bridge across Oak Creek. It took quite a while to finish so after we moved, my father helped finish. The first foot bridge was built by Uncle Frank Thompson, possibly others. It was located just above the car crossing and was strung from one big sycamore tree to another. It was rather hard to climb the steps up the tree on each side and down again. Before the new bridge was done, Paul and I used it to go to school. The new bridge was up the Creek and went from the McBride's across to the Purtymun's. At times in the summer, people crossed boards from one big rock to another in the creek bottom. In the late 80s or early 90s, after both Albert Purtymun and Albert Thompson had died and Clara had moved, Laura was forced to have the bridge taken down. A man had mentioned suing her if he was hurt on it. My husband helped her take it down.

Turning Back the Pages of Time II

We needed furniture for our house. We bought a second hand cook stove from Flagstaff. Uncle Guy, Ray McBride and Uncle Ab came to help unload and set it up in the kitchen. Later, we got a wood heater for the living room from Aunt Gertrude.

Paul helped get the old black sofa from the house Fred slept in, and he and Dad spent the morning cleaning and overhauling it. A kitchen table was taken from the upper house and chairs from the main house. In early May, my father bought plates in Flagstaff and moved other kitchen supplies to the canyon home.

That spring, Dad cleared a spot for the chicken house and used the loads of lumber he brought to build it. First, he cleared rocks and brush from the area, not far from the present gate on the north side of the road. He got the walls up and sheeting on and roofed it. Posts and holes were cut and dug for a chicken yard and were brought from Red Rock. Poles were put up for roosts and nests built. Sometimes, he made wooden eggs painted white to encourage hens to lay and Mom had a china egg. Little rocks were put on the floor. Some years later, the chicken house and yard were moved across the road, and a bigger yard was made and they are there now.

Charley Johnson, a friend of Sam's, gave him ducks he got at the Arizona State Fair. For a time, they were in a pen near the house. Hawks tried to get them. Later, a small house was made inside the back of the hen house and a pen and cement pond made. The land where the first house and pens had been was so rich, Dad had to remove some of the manure in the house area and put dirt in and leaves in before crops could be grown.

Dad hung doors in our house. We went to the old Sedona dump located off 89A across from Red Rock and got enough cardboard for a ceiling in one of the bedrooms. An earlier Sedona dump was behind the Brewer Road School on the dirt road that used to go from Sedona to Grasshopper Flats.

We needed an electric pump to irrigate so one was ordered in Clemenceau and electricity wire was purchased from the nearby R.E.A. office. Dad put electric wires over the house and strung them on a big oak tree between our house and the spring. Later, a metal pump shed was built for the electric pumps, a big one and a little one.

The last day we went to the Sedona School from Red Rock was Friday, May 21, 1948. The following Saturday morning, Paul went to get a drum of gas with Dad in Cottonwood. That afternoon, the family took gas, sacks of chicken feed and groceries to our ranch. We would need meat, so on Sunday they butchered a cow and hung it in the Jones' cooler.

We were sorry to learn that our old friend, Mrs. Owenby, had died. We weren't able to attend the funeral. We were busy moving chickens and other belongings. Before moving the chickens, they were caught; feathers cut off one wing and dusted for bugs. After we left, Fred had bad luck with his

Turning Back the Pages of Time II

chickens. A coon tore part of the roof off and came in and killed his chickens.

Before we moved, Paul got to attend a Junior Deputy picnic. He had joined, along with some classmates, in October of 1947.

The day after the chickens were moved, Albert Purtymun moved our two milk cows and calf in his new truck. Beginning early, we took up two more loads and stayed our first night on Dad's homestead. That day, Friday, May 29, was an especially happy one for Dad, to be returning home after over 10 years at Red Rock. Fred was almost 21 and could care for his ranch.

The day we moved, Mom, little Sam and I were riding in Fred's car and he was bringing a load over the hill. The road from the highway to our house was a narrow, one-lane road. To my sorrow, Fred killed the motor on the hill overlooking Munds Creek. He had no problem getting going again but I had visions of ending up in the Creek. Dad, and later on, Sam, made it wider, especially at the top of the hill. Years later, I drove our International Travel Van between the tractor and creek at the top of the hill.

The men had been hauling loads since May 21st. I was terribly disappointed when they refused to take my "precious" books until later. Fred spent our first night with us. The next morning, the boys and I rose early and got a nice mess of fish and more loads were hauled. Thus ended our days at Red Rock. It took a time to adjust to not being able to take off and walk in any direction and less sunshine, but I got used to it and it became home.

PORCH AREA OF MUNDS CREEK HOME (ELLEN, PAUL & SAM)

Turning Back the Pages of Time II

A

A Cowboy's Wife 129
Alhambra Phoenix School............13
Archebeau, Mrs..............................13
Arches of Time 5, 7
Arizona Highway Department 11, 53, 130
Arizona Power Company .. 108, 114
Arizona Public Service.................113
Armijo, Ambrosio 30

B

Bacon Rind Park 6, 27
Baker Billy.....................................151
Baker Family.................. 90, 91, 132
Baker Houdi..................................147
Baker, Houdie 90
Baldwin, Andrew 73
Baldwin, Andrew and Jane 66, 108, 123
Baldwin's 76, 84, 85, 86, 99, 108, 110, 111, 115, 117, 126, 146, 149, 155
Banjo Bill Campground 80
Barnes, Wayne 83
Barney Pasture 88
Bear Wallow 5
Beaver Head 90
Bedside Manor 8
Bee Canyon 96
Bell Rock 61
Big Park.....23, 77, 90, 92, 107, 108, 111, 117, 122, 128
Big Park road 23
Bird, Gene....................... 17, 19, 20
Births in 1937 66
Black Family..................................26
Black, Dora Parker........................26
Black, Ed 23, 24, 26, 27, 138
Black, Frances....................... 26, 27
Black, George 23, 91, 111
Black, Helen 28
Black, Mrs. George............... 76, *See* Hudspeth, Sally
Black, Sally..............................14, 80
Blaugh, Anita.................34, 45, 122
Blough, Albert 79
Boswell, Cora Mae and Paul........28
Boughton, Charley 69
Bougton..118
Bouton....................4, 76, 85, 86, 92
Bouton, Tina and Charley 73
Brewer Family 15, 17, 26, 55, 77
Brewer Lovella 19
Brewer Ollie 22
Brewer Road School 21, 23, 158
Brewer, Lydia 15, 18, 22
Bridgeport 13, 70, 84, 108, 112
Bristow, Allan 56
Brown, Carl 123
Brown, Dafne 123, 125
Burrus Family 146

C

Call of the Canyon......................130
Camp Verde 59, 83
Carlson, Doctor 80
Carroll Canyon . 84, 85, 86, 99, 102, 126, 149
CCC camp 24, 33
Chavez 11, 29, 30, 85, 101, 115, 119, 122, 124
Chavez crossing............................11
Chavez Ranch...............................86
Chavez, Ambrosio 77
Chavez, Dora and Ambrocito 45
Chipmunk Store 76
Christmas 15, 20, 41, 43, 44, 45, 48, 50, 54, 55, 57, 59, 69, 94, 104, 125, 139, 148
Circus......................................96, 97, 133
Clarkdale 37, 39, 45, 72, 75, 78, 79, 80, 128, 134, 141, 149
Clarkdale High School 78
Clemenceau 97, 158
Cole, Ben 84

Coleman, Emma Jean 20
Coleman, Fred and Vernon .. 14, 16, 20
Cook, Gene 77, 117, 152
Copple, Ben 79
Cottonwood . 13, 19, 27, 57, 67, 73, 76, 81, 83, 84, 112, 113, 114, 118, 123, 128, 129, 131, 134, 141, 145, 152, 158
Cottonwood Cemetery 134
Cottonwood Hospital 80, 129
Cottonwood, Jail 128
Court, Van 130
Crescent Moon Ranch . 66, 124, 155
Croxen, Edith .... 55, *Also See* Teachers:Lamport, Edith

D

Dalton, Jack 122
Delanio, Franklin 26
Depression 24
Despain, Wendel 42, 122
Dickins, Donald 77
Dickinson, Aaron 77
Dickison, Kelly 117
Dietricks 120, 121
Doney Park 93, 108, 112
Dumas, Doc 56
Dumas' House 123
Duncan, Nick 124

E

Easter egg hunt 44
Elmer Family 5, 45, 54, 74, 82, 109, 121, 123, 137, 138, 151, 152
Elmer, Dorothy 35
Elmer, Jessie 74
Elmer, Justin 35, 40, 47, 49
Elmer,Jay Sr. 74
Elmersville 131, 132
Etter, Clyde 109, 110

F

Falls School 89
fire 15, 74, 84, 88

Ellen Graves

Flagstaff .. 15, 16, 20, 21, 23, 25, 28, 48, 54, 71, 74, 76, 77, 80, 82, 87, 96, 97, 108, 112, 118, 122, 131, 133, 134, 135, 140, 149, 150, 151, 157
Flagstaff Airport 93
flood 4, 7, 8, 9, 10, 11, 86, 102, 116, 126
Flood, Leo 26
Fox, Morley 113
Fuentez, Ed 109

G

Gaddis, Charley 121
Garbarino, Mrs. 22
Gardening 71
Garland, Dora 28
Garland, William 28
Garrison, Ersel 118, 128
Gene, Sherman 90
Glenellen 67, 93
Graduating Class Sedona School 1993 22
Grand Canyon 21
Grasshopper Flats 13, 23, 80, 84, 90, 108, 109, 111, 119, 128, 131, 132, 152, 158
Grasshopper Point 9
Graves Children 21
Graves, Ellen Thompson 45, 49
Graves, Nelson 11, 28, 48, 49, 53, 54, 74, 85, 91, 133, 142
Graves, Ruth 22
Gray Mountain 90
Green, Mary Bell 130
Greenough Family 72
Greenwell Family 95, 96, 112

H

Halloween 18, 19, 41, 42, 47, 50, 51, 89
Hardy Boys 20, 139
Hart, Dad and Mrs. 23, 24
Hart, Fred and Nellie 9
Hart, Fred family 6
Hart, Nelly Mae 130

Turning Back the Pages of Time II

Hart's Store 23, 24, 138, 141
Hedges 9, 137
Hedges, Red 26
Hedges, Rube 147
Hedges, Vera Purtymun.................4
Hi Low Ranch..................... 120, 122
Highway 89A 7, 24
Hoel, Don...................................26
Hollamon, Louise 39, 45
Hollomond, Ann Louise 123
Hollomond, Otto 109, 119, 121
Hollomond, Sally .... 121, *also See* Teachers
Huckaby, Nathan..........................30
Hudspeth, Georgia 14, 111
Hudspeth, Sally 13

I

Indian children 21
Indian Garden Bridge.....................5
Indian Gardens ... 4, 6, 7, 11, 13, 15, 25, 28, 39, 81, 86, 92, 112, 119, 126, 131, 151, 153

J

Jackson ... 13, 14, 15, 16, 22, 23, 25, 27, 28, 51, 138, 139
    Frank 23
Jackson School 14
Jackson, Ed 26
Jackson, Frank 13, 14, 16, 23, 24, 25, 26, 27, 28
Jackson, James 13
Jackson, James A..........................13
Jackson, Ruth Jordan ....*See* Jordan, Ruth
Jackson, Wesley . 13, 15, 16, 26, 28, 139
Jay Cook's farm 150
Jerome 17, 108, 124, 129, 132, 134, 139
Johnson, Charley 61, 157
Jones, Albert and Janie 69
Jones, Claire 40, 48, 57, 65, 73, 120, 123, 126, 148, 154

Jones, Grace Kurtz 65
Jones, James 35, 39, 40, 67, 108, 120, 152
Jones, Paul 54
Jones, Stephen..........................141
Jordan Family 17, 18, 19, 40, 41, 47, 48, 50, 60, 75, 105, 108, 137
Jordan Ruth 49
Jordan, Helen 16, 18
Jordan, Ruth. 16, 17, 18, 40, 46, 47, 49, 51
Jordan, Walter 34, 40, 47, 48, 49
Junipine 7

K

Keith, Cleve 109, 123
Keith, Stella 123
Kipina, Geraldine 27
Kittridge, Bob 110
Kurtz, Gertrude 123
Kurtz, Roy 77

L

Lay, Dave 92
Lay, Joe 148
Lay, Joe and Inez 57
LeMay, Barbara 54
Leupp..21
Leyel, Mattie 83
Lofton 113
Lowell Observatory.....................48
Lower Loop Road 121, 122
Loy ... 5, 34, 40, 45, 47, 77, 122, 132
Loy Canyon 91
Loy, Frieda (Schuerman)...........120
Loy, Martha 34, 39, 42
Loy, Myron (Budge) ..34, 69, 75, 76, 109, 120
Loy, Sherman 9, 45, 74, 90, 132
Lyndalls...............................121, 127

M

Manzanita campground 7
Martinez Family 121

163

Martinez, Alahandro..........121, 122
McBride.. 8, 16, 67, 76, 81, 95, 111, 151, 153, 156
McBride Ted................................133
McBride, Dave..................................8
McBride, Family............................66
McBride, Gwen 89, 91
McBride, Laura and Ray................10
McBride, Laura Purtymun ..6, 7, 10, 83, 89, 104, 109, 153
McBride, Ray 89, 104, 109, 110, 156, 157
McBride, Ted....................19, 89, 91
McDonald, Dr. and Mrs. 36
McDowell 8
Mercer, Earl 93
Mercer, Pearl 93
Michael, Chester 81
Midgley Bridge 5
Miller Family .. 22, 30, 35, 110, 111, 112
Miller George 113
Miller, Hazel 22
Miller, Ralph 22
Mission Rancho..............................7
Mongeni Family 70
Montezuma Castle.......................97
Montgomery Family 66
Montgomery, Mike........66, 67, 130
Morrison, Fred 109, 112, 113
Mosley, Bud 16
Munds Creek 4, 6, 10, 55, 103, 106, 142, 155, 159
Munds Park.....................5, 10, 146
Myers, Susan................................21

N

Nancy Drew..........................20, 139

O

Oak Creek 4, 5, 6, 10, 13, 45, 46, 59, 80, 85, 86, 92, 96, 99, 108, 109, 111, 112, 113, 115, 116, 121, 128, 130, 131, 133, 156
Old Red Rock Road 120
Olson, Merle 80

Orpheum Theatre......................133
Owenby.. 80, 84, 92, 122, 125, 126, 132, 147, 154, 158
Owenby Ranch...........................106
Owenby, Getha and Dorothy 45
Owenby, Roy...79, 80, 86, 114, 121, 124

P

Page Springs Road 111, 131, 152
Parker, Denver.............................26
Passmore, Betty...........................19
Peach Springs..............................69
Pearl Harbor 73
Pelekeske, Sue 21
Pendley 8, 26, 108
Pendley Bridge..............................8
Pendley Ranch 89
Pendley, Frank 46
Pendley, Tom 77
Pendley's Cabins 130
Pesky Calf 119
Pine Flats.....................26, 76, 138
Piper Family 6, 77
Piper Lee 147
Pirtle, Gene 20
Poco Diablo 23
Poor Farm 23
Possee Grounds 137
Purtymun Emory 139
Purtymun Family 137, 138, 151, 156, 159
Purtymun, Ab............................156
Purtymun, Albert.......118, 131, 156
Purtymun, Bud.....5, 7, 77, 104, 117
Purtymun, Chester 77
Purtymun, Clara Thompson ... 7, 29, 55
Purtymun, Elmer 54, 109
Purtymun, Jesse....................7, 131
Purtymun, Laura ....*See* McBride, Laura Purtymun
Purtymun, Lizzie 4
Purtymun, Vera Hedges ..... *Hedges, Vera Purtymun*

Turning Back the Pages of Time II

Q

Quick, Tom 8

R

Rainbow Bridge 91
Rainbows End 129
Ramarez Family 122
Ray McBride 111
REA....108, 109, 110, 111, 112, 113, 114, 133
Red Rock 5, 9, 16, 18, 19, 21, 24, 28, 30, 33, 37, 40, 42, 45, 46, 47, 49, 51, 57, 58, 59, 61, 65, 66, 67, 69, 74, 75, 87, 88, 97, 99, 100, 102, 103, 106, 108, 111, 112, 113, 114, 117, 118, 120, 122, 124, 125, 126, 127, 129, 130, 131, 132, 134, 138, 139, 146, 152,154, 155, 157, 158, 159
Red Rock Crossing 85, 124, 155
Red Rock Farms 74
Red Rock Ladies 124
Red Rock News 56
Red Rock Road 90, 148
Red Rock School. 14, 29, 37, 49, 83, 89, 120
Redman, John 113
Rhore, Steve 156
Rialto Theatre 128, 133
Riggins, Effie 153
Road, Sedona to Red Rock 69
Robbins, Bob and Virginia 75
Robbins, Carol 39
Route 66 93
Rupe, Bill 93
Rupe, Violet 93
Russell, Burrell 81, 92, 117
Russell, Dick 4, 10
Russell, Lawton 107, 152

S

Schnebly Family 17
Schnebly Hill Road 146
Schnebly Sedona 18
Schnebly T.C. 24
Schuerman 2, 29, 40, 47, 69, 90, 118, 120, 121, 123, 132, 144
Schuerman Mountain..90, 118, 121
Schuerman, Dolly 17, 121
Schuerman, Doretta and Henry 9
Schuerman, Erwin....29, 59, 65, 120
Schuerman, Family 45, 120
Schuerman, Fred......4, 9, 11, 42, 45, 74, 113
Schuerman, Fritz 79, 121
Schuerman, Henrietta 34, 39, 40, 47, 139
Schuerman, Henry 29, 40, 69, 99, 109, 114, 117, 120, 144, 154
Schuerman, Jewel 92, 120, 124
Schuerman, Lanora..........39, 47, 82
Sedona . 6, 9, 11, 15, 16, 18, 19, 21, 23, 24, 25, 27, 28, 46, 69, 71, 73, 75, 76, 88, 97, 101, 108, 109, 119, 121, 125, 128, 131, 137, 139, 141, 150, 152
Sedona Assembly of God Church 138
Sedona Bridge 9
Sedona Dump 158
Sedona Heritage Museum 105
Sedona High School 90
Sedona School.... 13, 14, 17, 18, 19, 20, 21, 22, 29, 55, 89, 158
skating rink.....................25, 28, 92
Skikee .... *See* Delanio, Franklin
Slide Rock 26
Smelter City 134, 141
Smith, Else 131
Smith, Ernie 113
Smith, Ira 5, 129, 131
Smith, Mary .... *See* Wyatt, Mary
Snowball (Dog) 70
Spring Creek Ranch 72
St. George, Utah ..... 11, 52, 53, *also See* Utah, Northern
Sugar Loaf 90
Sullivan, Melena *See* West, Bill and Lena

T

Table Mountain 101
Taylor, Doctor 66, 67
Taylor, Russell 45, 113
Teachers
    Alfred Wohslegel 15
    Baker, Miss 21
    Bird, Oma 17
    Bunger 15
    Carter, Vance 21
    Clark, Ellen 20
    Cortez, Grace 30
    Daliy, Sylvia 21
    Davis, Mary Lee 35
    Daweson, Henrietta 30
    Ellen Grant 15
    Fall, Marion 42
    Fisher, Thelma 21
    Freestone 15
    Greene 15
    Guthine, Garey H. 30
    Hance, Josephine 30
    Hotchkiss, Dotty 20
    James, Wanda 21
    Jolly, V. 30
    Jordan, Ruth .... *See* Jordan Ruth
    Kelsey, Don 21
    Kline, John 21
    Lamport, Edith 20, 55, 56
    Mason, Peggy 21
    Matty Evans 15
    Maxwell, Minnie 29
    McGookin, Arnes 46
    Mumford, Gladys 20
    Nefstead, Kriss 21
    Nichols, Julie 30
    Nicklen, Abby 39
    Olsen, Mrs. 17
    Owenby, Alta 30
    Price, Lois 17
    Reed, Charlotte 30
    Riordan . 15, 16, 17, 20, 21, 139, 140
    Riordan, Elsie 121
    Robbins, Virgie 35, 37
    Schuerman, Dolly 30
    Sides, Venda 16
    Smith, Priscilla 45
    Stemmer, Charley 20
    Taylor, Mr. 21
    Wallace, Stanton 17
    Ward, A. 30
    West, Mr. 21
    Wohslegel, Alfred 15
    Worst, Lily 30
The High Low Ranch 92
Thompson.6, 10, 16, 17, 22, 27, 28, 29, 40, 47, 55, 67, 94, 132, 137, 145
Thompson Family 2, 23, 25, 34
Thompson Ladder 8
Thompson Road 95
Thompson, Aaron 21
Thompson, Albert 20, 30, 46, 120
Thompson, Avis 9, 22, 66, 89
Thompson, Charley .. 6, 8, 9, 55, 66, 89, 110, 137, 152
Thompson, Charlotte Ruth 28
Thompson, Claude 20
Thompson, Dave James 57
Thompson, Frank 8, 75, 121, 151, 156
Thompson, Fred 29, 81, 156
Thompson, Gertrude 150
Thompson, Gloria 20, 28
Thompson, Greene and Gertrude
    10
Thompson, Guy 25, 28, 81, 151
Thompson, Guy and Greene 14
Thompson, Hilda 8, 9, 75, 151
Thompson, Jack 75
Thompson, Jim 25, 28, 81, 91
Thompson, Lee 94
Thompson, Mabel 56
Thompson, Margaret 28
Thompson, Morgan 23
Thompson, Paul 45
Thompson, Paula 21
Thompson, Roy 39
Thompson, Sam 61, 82, 83
Thompson, Samantha 21
Tines, Rex 113
Tlaquepaque 6
Towne, Bill and Gwen 11
Trout Farm 11

Turning Back the Pages of Time II

U

Utah, Northern 52

V

Valentine 41, 50
Van Deren. 5, 16, 18, 20, 22, 55, 67, 137
Van Deren Family 138
Van Deren, Beverly 19
Van Deren, Lee 23
Van Deren, Maggie 4
Van Deren, Walter 19
Verde Bridge 13
Verde Hot Springs 79, 108
Verde River 13, 66, 131
Verde Valley ... 25, 79, 97, 108, 122, 125, 133
Verde Valley Lumber Co. 134
Verde Valley School 90, 99
Vest, Roy 130

W

water 5, 6, 7, 8, 9, 11, 33, 36, 50, 71, 84, 85, 87, 88, 92, 97, 102, 103, 104, 107, 108, 114, 115, 116, 126, 149
Wentworth, Mrs. 39, 122
West Family 59
West Sedona 13, 18, 21, 91
West, Bill and Lena 58, 59
West, Jimmy 58, 59
Wester, Orville 20
Whitcome Family 121
White Flats . 90, 117, 129, 130, 131, 154
Wickenburg 13, 97
Wickenburg School 13
Willard school 13
Wilson Mountain 7, 91
Winona 93
WORLD WAR II 3, 73
Wright, Ned 76
Wyatt, Mary 7, 9, 129, 130
Wyatt, Smiley 131

Z

Zane Grey 20, 139

Back Cover: *Guy Thompson, Man in apron is father of Carol, Eleanor, Janet, Jim (Guy's brother) – Indian Gardens, J.J. Thompson Ranch*